A Prac
Guide to Early Years Education

by

Dame Kate Dethridge

A John Catt Publication

First Published 2016

by John Catt Educational Ltd,
12 Deben Mill Business Centre, Old Maltings Approach,
Melton, Woodbridge IP12 1BL

Tel: +44 (0) 1394 389850 Fax: +44 (0) 1394 386893
Email: enquiries@johncatt.com
Website: www.johncatt.com

ISBN: 978 1 911382 13 3

Set and designed by John Catt Educational Limited

About the Author

Dame Kate Dethridge has spent over 30 years in primary education. She started as an early years teacher and this has remained a passion throughout her career. As an additional Ofsted inspector and headteacher of an outstanding teaching school and national support school, she has inspected and supported countless settings. It has allowed her to learn from the best, developing a detailed understanding of what excellent provision looks like and how it is both established and maintained. She was made a dame in Her Majesty's 2015 New Year's honours for services to education.

"This is a guide for passionate practitioners, written by a particularly expert and passionate practitioner. It both explains the practical details of promoting different areas of learning but also offers detailed advice on assessment, safeguarding and inspection. A must for all who believe that the answer to improving social mobility is getting it right in children's early years."
Dr Tim Coulson, Regional Schools Commissioner for the East of England

"This book is an excellent introduction for those new to EYFS and a great guide for those wishing to develop their knowledge of the sector further. Its clarity, rooted in effective practice and systems, is a valuable addition to any teacher's, or indeed parent's, reading list."
Simon Knight, director of education, the National Education Trust

"A useful and easy read for early years practitioners. It supports the adage that, 'a reflective practitioner is an effective practitioner' and provides many audits and reflective tools that can be used by leaders to monitor and develop pedagogy, practice and provision with early years teams."
Clare Kershaw, Head of Commissioning Education and Lifelong Learning at Essex County Council

"If both experienced and new leaders want really good practical advice about how to establish highly effective EYFS provision, then they should read this book."
Helena Mills, CEO of Burnt Mill Academy Trust

Contents

Introduction

Early years education plays a crucial role in ensuring children make the best possible start in life, developing their confidence, interests and ensuring they establish the social skills and attitudes to learning that they require to succeed at school. Get it right in the early years and children are set up for life. It is a huge privilege to be involved in such a significant stage of children's lives but with this comes great responsibility. Some of us are lucky enough to have the opportunity to visit many excellent settings and learn from them; we see highly effective practice and duplicate it. For those who are unable to make such visits, a book of lessons learned is the next best thing.

A Practical Guide to Early Years Education has been written in order to support colleagues in gaining an understanding of what excellent provision looks like, offering tools and resources to help you manage, improve and sustain high quality provision in your setting. Pick up a book about early years education and too often it is heavily weighted with research and theory. These are important elements but for many of us who are busy and short on time, we simply want to be able to open a book and find it full of good ideas with easily accessible resources that are easy to read and written by someone who does the job every day. Whether you are a child minder or work in a nursery school, this book will offer you sensible and practical advice about what you can do to improve the experience for the children in your care, meeting their individual needs and sustain improved learning outcomes.

Written in a clear and easily accessible way, each chapter focuses on a key area of provision and offers a wealth of practical ideas and resources to help you:

- Understand what excellent provision looks like and should include.
- Audit your own provision to identify strengths and areas to improve.
- Develop resources and guidance for staff to ensure that your setting offers all the necessary support and skills to guarantee the children in your care make progress, are stimulated and develop excellent attitudes to learning.

Whether you need a better understanding of the needs of children acquiring English as an additional language, improve your outdoor provision or ensure your safeguarding practices are effective and compliant, this book will support you and ensure that you have a comprehensive understanding of what needs to be improved and how you can easily achieve this. Each chapter addresses the crucial areas of learning in early years settings and, in addition, will help you consider how to develop key workers, how to confirm children are 'school ready' and how to prepare for and succeed when being inspected.

The book offers advice and strategies for establishing highly effective behaviour management strategies, how to engage boys and plan a curriculum that appeals to them, as well as giving tips and guidance on making observations to develop effective assessment practice. In addition, there is a chapter dedicated to leadership in early years settings which identifies expectations and offers support in ensuring any setting is well-led and managed. This is a book is for educators and leaders alike to inform your practice while offering quick, easy and sustainable tools for self-assessment and improvement.

I hope this book will give you the understanding, confidence and tools to improve your own provision and that it will provide a catalyst for debate and discussion. I would like to thank all those people I have met and settings I have visited that have improved my own understanding of excellent early years provision. In this book, I share their skills and ideas in the hope that all children will benefit from excellent provision to sustain them through their childhood and beyond.

Children's language: oracy and literacy

Language learning through interaction

Modelling: The role of the adults

Speaking and listening are the two essential tools of all children in their quest to understand, communicate and participate with the world and with others. In order to become good readers and writers, children must develop good speech and communication skills first. Whilst incidental use of language and conversation are obviously vital parts of an effective early years setting, adults must also plan for the acquisition of language. Given how crucial it is, it cannot be left to chance. Children have to be given the opportunity to talk in a variety of settings and this needs to be planned for and resourced. The role of the adult is undeniably crucial, they must plan, model, encourage and listen.

Planning

It is important to question whether you provide opportunities every day for children to speak to other children and adults. At the end of each day, are you able to say that you have had a conversation with every child in your setting or for those whom you are responsible for as a key worker? This is something you should regularly check. When introducing a new theme or topic with the children, do you identify some of the new vocabulary that you will be using? In addition to this, practitioners should plan for opportunities to model words. This allows children to become familiar with them, understand their meaning, rehearse it and apply the words accurately.

Modelling language

Children learn by example and so practitioners must model the language and conventions they wish the children to use. Adults in an early years setting are not there purely in a supervisory role. They have an essential part to play interacting with children.

They do this by:

1. Developing vocabulary

Introduce new words that have a meaning to the children, words that they can use and apply every day. These words can be based on the daily routine of the children or linked to the topic you are studying. The introduction of vocabulary needs to be planned and staff must create opportunities both to model new words and for children to rehearse the use of them in context.

2. Engaging children in conversation

The adult in a child's life is the chief resource in language development. Children also learn a great deal from each other, but largely much of their learning will be via the adults who spend time with them. As teachers, we need to ensure that we engage children in conversation, listen carefully to them and ask open-ended questions that require more than a one-word answer. It is important to respond to what children say to us and sustain their language development and growth. We must also regularly raise our expectation of the level of sophistication and vocabulary that they employ.

The best practitioners do the following instinctively:

Speaking

- Offer a narrative to children about what they are doing or what is happening in the setting. This does not need to be done repetitively as children will need an opportunity to process what is being said to them too.
- Show how to use language to communicate with others, share their feelings and ask questions. This can be done both by modelling the process and by highlighting to children how their peers use language efficiently.
- Model the facial expressions involved in making conversation, for example looking surprised or asking questions. For very young children, these expressions may need to be exaggerated so that they understand the link between what is being said and what somebody is feeling. The ability to interpret language not only verbally but also visually is a critical skill which young children need to acquire.
- Model the use of new vocabulary and encourage children to use it within an appropriate context.
- Use physical actions in tandem with language so that children are able to see the link between actions and language. Try to explain to the children why you are doing something, for example as you put your coat on you might say to a child, "come on, it's time for us to put our coats on because we are going outside".
- Treat children as conversationalists even if they are not saying very much.

Listening

- Stop what you are doing and give the child your full attention.
- Get down to their level so that you can make eye contact.

- Wait until they have finished what they want to say before you offer a response.
- Avoid interrupting or rushing them.

If we want children to listen to others then we must model the conventions of good listening ourselves.

All activities in the early years setting offer opportunities to develop, understand and extend language for children. For practitioners, it is worth considering which activities lend themselves to developing a particular area of language development:

Activity	Purpose	Role of adult
Songs and rhymes	Extending a child's stamina for paying attention and listening.	Children become familiar with words and phrases and can join in easily, improving their confidence. Regular repetition of songs and rhymes, including actions, read in an enthusiastic and meaningful way. Children enjoy, predict and join in. Introduce clapping games where you clap a rhythm and the child has to copy the pattern.
Interactive story telling	Children become familiar with story conventions.	Tell stories in an exciting way, offering children opportunities to repeat, predict, tell parts themselves and finish sentences with familiar phrases.
Small world activities	Encourage imaginative play alongside their peers. Develop communication skills and apply vocabulary and phrases learned.	Select appropriate small world toys that support prior learning. Encourage children to apply vocabulary and phrases, play alongside children, modelling phrases, questions, actions.
Feely bags	Encourages children to develop descriptive vocabulary. Develops confidence to speak to others.	Ask open-ended questions that encourage descriptive language from children. Model the use of particular vocabulary so children can see how it is used in context.
Sand and water play	Develop children's ability to describe actions, sensations and the properties of both sand and water. This is a great opportunity to develop the understanding of how to use prepositions.	Create play opportunities that ensure children begin to understand the meaning of prepositions in a very real context, e.g. 'pour the water through/ over/ on top of..." This can also introduce the vocabulary of measurement.
Role-play	Role-play can offer children the opportunity to understand and use the conventions of conversation. It builds confidence in communicating with others and verbalising ideas and thoughts.	Create a stimulating and familiar environment that the children feel comfortable in. If the role-play is linked to storytelling or areas of the curriculum that they are already familiar with then they feel more confident about engaging and speaking because they have begun to acquire the necessary vocabulary. Adults should also be involved in the role-play themselves so that they can model behaviours and ideas to children.

Use of technology, such as microphones, video recorders, CD players	Young children can be very excited about using technology and, in particular, seeing and hearing their recorded voices played back to them.	Show children how to use the technology, whilst allowing independence. Be a receptive audience to the recorded sound and/or vision. Think of creative ways to use technology that supports the topic being studied and engages all children, e.g. making video diaries, creating short plays for an audience, giving children microphones so that they can role-play singing or interviewing.

It is essential to plan for and encourage interaction between children and their peers. Peer learning is an important part of language development, in both your planned adult-led activities and the group play with their peers so do try to nurture collaboration and discussion. Be mindful of any children who are very quiet and spend a great deal of time playing alone. Whilst there is nothing wrong with this in itself, children do need to be encouraged to socialise and communicate with their peers.

It is useful to regularly assess a child's language development, however young they may be. It is important to judge whether children are failing to meet, are meeting or exceeding particular milestones. Although a delay can be a cause for concern, we also need to remember that children develop at a variety of ages and stages. Assessments are best if they include input from families too.

This assessment tool from Surrey County Council is something that many nurseries and early years settings have found useful:

Early Language Child Monitoring Tools

Name: ______________________ **Dob:** ____________ **Age in months:** ________

Date	Date	Date	Date	Date	Date
Age	Age	Age	Age	Age	Age

Stage	Listening & Attention	Understanding (Receptive Language)	Talking (Expressive Language)	Social Communication
0-11 months	Turns toward a familiar sound then locates range of sounds with accuracy. Listens to, distinguishes and responds to intonations and sounds of voices. Grows quiet or alerts to the sound of speech. Fleeting attention – not under child's control, new stimuli takes whole attention.	Stops and looks when they hear their own name (by 12 months). Starts to understand contextual clues, e.g. familiar gestures, words and sounds.	To communicate to adults: says sounds like 'baba', 'nana' and 'gaga' (by 11 months). Communicates needs and feelings in a variety of ways including crying, gurgling, billing and squealing. Lifts arms in anticipation of being picked up.	Gazes at face and copies facial movements e.g. sticking out tongue. Concentrates intently on faces and enjoys interaction. To make contact with people and keep their attention (by 12 months).

8-20 months	Concentrates intently on an object or activity of own choosing for short periods. Pays attention to dominant stimulus – easily distracted by noises or other people talking. Moves whole bodies to sounds they enjoy, such as music or a regular beat Has a strong exploratory impulse.	Developing the ability to follow others' body language, including pointing and gesture. Responds to the different things said when in a familiar context with a special person (e.g. 'Where's Mummy?' and 'Where's your nose?'). Understanding of single words in context is developing, e.g. 'cup', 'milk', 'daddy'.	Uses single words (by 16 months). Frequently imitates words and sounds. Enjoys babbling and increasingly experiments with using sounds and words to represent objects.	Likes being with familiar adults and watching them. Developing the ability to follow an adult body language, including pointing gestures. Learns that their voice and actions have effects on others. Uses pointing with I gaze to make requests, and to share an interest (by 18 months).
16-25 months	Listens to and enjoys rhythmic patterns in rhymes and stories Enjoys rhythm and demonstrates listening by trying to join in with actions or vocalisations rigid attention – may appear not to hear	Selects familiar objects by name and will go and find objects when asked or identify objects from a group. Understand simple sentences (e.g. throw the ball).	Starts to put two words together (e.g. want ball, more juice) (by 24 months). Uses different types of everyday words (verbs and adjectives, e.g. go sleep, hot, big). Beginning to ask simple questions.	Gradually able to engage in 'pretend' play with toys (support child to imagine another's point of view). Looks to others for responses that confirm, contribute to or challenge their understanding.
22-36 months	Single-channel detention. Can shift to a different task if attention fully obtained; using child's name helps focus (by 36 months). Listens with interest to the noises adults make when they read stories. Recognises and responds to many familiar sounds, e.g. turning to a knock at the door, looking at or going to the door.	Identifies action words by pointing to the right picture e.g. who is jumping? (By 30 months) Understands who, what, where in simple questions (e.g. who's that where is…?). Developing understanding of simple concepts e.g. big/little).	Learns new words very rapidly and is able to use them in communicating. Uses action, sometimes with limited talk, that is largely concerned with the 'here and now' (e.g. reaches toward toy, saying 'I have it'). Uses a variety of questions (e.g. what, when, who). Uses simple sentences (e.g.' Mummy going work') Beginning to use word endings.	Uses language as a powerful means of widening contacts, sharing feelings, experiences and thoughts. Holds a conversation, jumping from topic to topic. Enjoys being with and talking to adults and other children. Interested in others' play and will join in. Responds to the feelings of others.

30-50 months	Listens to others in one to one or small groups, when conversation interests them. Listens to stories with increasing attention and recall. Joins in with repeated refrains and anticipates key events and phrases in rhymes and stories. Focusing their attention – still listens, but can shift their own attention. Is able to follow directions (if not intently focused on own choice of activity).	Understands use of objects (e.g. 'What do we use to cut things?'). Shows understanding of prepositions such as 'under', 'on top', 'behind' by carrying out an action or selecting correct picture. Beginning to understand 'why' and 'how' questions.	Beginning to use more complex sentences (e.g. using and, because). Can retell a simple past event in correct order (e.g. went down slide, hurt finger). Uses talk to connect ideas, explain what is happening and anticipate what might happen next, recall and relive past experiences. Questions why things happen and give explanations. Asks who, what, when. Uses a range of tenses (e.g. play, playing, will play, played).	Beginning to accept the needs of others, with support. Can initiate conversations. Shows confidence in linking up with others for support and guidance. Talks freely about their home and community. Forms friendships with other children.
40-60 months	Sustains attentive listening, responding to what they have heard with relevant comments, questions or actions. Maintains attention, concentrates and sits quietly when appropriate. Two-channeled attention – they can listen and do for short span. Integrated attention – can listen and do in range of situations with range of people; varies according to the demands of the task.	Understands humor, e.g. nonsense rhymes, jokes. Demonstrates understanding of "how?" and "why?" questions by giving explanations. Able to follow a story without pictures or props. Understands instructions containing sequencing words; first...after... last, and more abstract concepts – long, short, tall, hard soft, rough.	Extends vocabulary, especially by grouping and naming, exploring the meaning and sounds of new words. Links statements and sticks to a main theme or intention. Uses language to imagine and recreate roles and experiences in play situations. Uses talk to organise, sequence and clarify thinking, ideas, feelings and events. Introduces a storyline or narrative into their play.	Has confidence to speak to others about their own wants, interests and opinions. Initiates conversation, attends to and takes account of what others say. Explains own knowledge and understanding, asks appropriate questions of others. Shows awareness of the listener when speaking. Expresses needs or feelings in appropriate ways. Forms good relationships with adults and peers. Works as part of a group or class, taking turns.

50-72 months	Listens and changes focus of their attention independently and is starting to ignore unimportant information. Listens and follows more complex instructions such as, "finish your picture, then choose a story, and then sit on the carpet". Listens and maintains attention in a group situation for an increasing length of time when directed.	Understands and predicts what is happening in a story Understands that the same two words can mean two different things e.g. 'see' and 'sea'. Understands more abstract concepts like feelings and descriptive words such as, 'carefully', 'slowly', or 'clever' and uses them appropriately. Understands and answers more complex questions about the past and future such as, "what did you do yesterday?"	Uses language to persuade and negotiate or question. Uses language to predict and draw conclusions. Can guess the word from clues or give others clues using shape, size and function	Uses and experiments with different language such as current peer language. Beginning to be aware of what the listener already knows and checks e.g. "you know where I live, right? Well, in the big house by the shop...." Realises that people can experience different emotions to the same event.

Ref: Surrey County Council: Early Language Child Monitoring Tool

Stage	**Speech sounds (Developing speech and being understood applies to all languages. Order of acquiring specific sounds – here in English – may vary with other languages)**
0-11 months	They babble, using a range of sound combinations with changes in pitch, rhythm and loudness. They babble with intonation and rhythm of their home language, known as 'jargon'.
8-20 months	Their speech consists of a combination of jargon and some real words that may be difficult to understand.
16-25 months	They may use many immature speech patterns so speech may not be clear. They may leave out last sounds or substitute sounds, for example 'tap' for 'cap'. Uses most vowels and the sounds of letters such as m,p,b,n,t,d,w and h.
22-36 months	Their speech is becoming clearer, and usually understood by others by 36 months, although some immature speech patterns will still be evident. They may still substitute sounds or leave out the last sound. Emerging sounds include the sounds of letters such as k,g,f,s,z,l and y.
30-50 months	Others can, for the most part, understand speech, even in connected speech. There is an emerging use of the sounds 'ng', 'sh', 'ch,' 'j', 'v', 'th' and r, which may be inconsistent. Sound clusters may start emerging, for example the 'pl' in play or the 'sm' in smile, though some may be simplified, such as 'gween' for 'green'.
40-60 months	They are now overall fully intelligible to others but may be still developing the sound of 'r' and 'th'. They may simplify complex clusters such as 'skr' or 'str'.

How do we ensure our environment encourages the development of language in young children?

The most important resource for developing children's language and oracy skills is the staff that interact with the children every day. It is absolutely crucial that leaders in settings invest heavily in ensuring that all staff members understand the importance of interaction with all children, whatever the child's age. They must be aware that the expectation is that they offer a dialogue or narrative and ask open-ended questions, modelling excellent language behaviours at all times. There are times that they may be slightly more passive. This can be when they are making observations about children or carefully listening to what a child is saying. As a general rule, practitioners should be involved with either speaking or listening carefully for the best part of each day. In the worst settings, practitioners stand back or remain virtually silent, even if they are next to children. Any such practice should be nipped in the bud quickly. Looking after young children well requires participation, anything less than this cannot be accepted.

Although staff are a key resource to developing language and oracy, this is very much supported by developing a language-rich environment. It is useful to regularly audit your environment to ensure that it supports your work in language development.

Literacy learning environment checklist

Providing a range of quality literacy experiences and a print-rich physical environment is an important factor in the facilitation and support of literacy learning. It may be useful to review the learning environment using the following guidelines:

	In place	Area for development	Comments
Environmental print: letters and words Is the setting bright, well organised and inviting to walk into? Are resources and working areas clearly labelled, including photographs? Do the resources reflect the range of families and cultures in Britain? Are children's names and high frequency words displayed at height the child can see at? Are greetings/days of the week displayed in English and other languages and scripts? Is there an attractive pictorial alphabet frieze displayed at a height the child can see at? Are poems, songs, children's writing and extracts from shared texts displayed? Do displays include typed and handwritten text? Does the teacher read and refer to the print that is displayed around the setting? Do displays include typed and handwritten text and captions from adults and children? Does each room have a core of good quality books recommended for that particular age range? Is there a good range of text types available, such as fiction and non-fiction? Do the outdoor areas have language open-ended questions, vocabulary and prepositions by the climbing apparatus and capacity vocabulary by the sand and water?			
	In place	Area for development	Comments
Opportunities for children to read independently and for adults to read with children Does reading and writing happen inside and outdoors in reception? Do adults read to the children every day? Are there lots of opportunities to hear, sing and discuss rhymes? Are the books easily visible to all the children during shared reading? Do children take an active role in group, shared and guided reading? Are the children building a good bank of known texts?			

	In place	Area for development	Comments
Books and literacy areas Do the books in the book corner match the needs and interests of the children? Are the books of appropriate quality, quantity and variety, such as hard cover/ soft cover books, fiction/non-fiction books and those with rhymes? Are Big Books, favourite and new books and phonics games available for independent use? Are books included in displays and are available resources related to other areas of learning, other than communication, language and literacy? Are there enough guided reading resources to meet the needs of reception? 20–30 titles are likely to be needed at book band pink level. Do the books for early reading have a repetitive structure? Do the books for early reading have text that includes the repetition of high frequency words? Do the books for early reading include a good proportion of words the children can decode using their phonic skills? For shared reading, is the type and page layout simple and clear so that the children can isolate known high frequency words? Are the texts short enough to be completed in a 10–15 minute shared reading session?			
	In place	Area for development	Comments
Early writing Do children see adults reading and writing for different purposes and in different contexts? Is there an appealing writing area that includes writing materials, high frequency word cards, interactive displays, messages, and examples of children's writing available for independent use? Indoors and out? Are there lots of different resources for writing (and mark-making in reception), such as large sheets of paper, boards, chalks, big brushes, pens and paper? Is there an inviting listening post with a variety of stories and rhymes on tape? Are puppets, props and small-world items available for role-play? Do the outside area in reception and the role-play area include opportunities for reading and writing, and has an adult modelled these? Is there enough floor space inside and outside for being dramatic and creative, e.g. acting out stories, making dens, working on large sheets of paper? Are children able to access physical development activities that will build their fine and gross motor skills, e.g. building wrist strength by twirling ribbon sticks, practising writing patterns with big brushes and water, making letters in the sand? Are there lots of opportunities to link language with physical movement, e.g. in action songs and rhymes, cookery, gardening? Do children have access to a computer and are there suitable reading and writing software programs in use? If there is an interactive whiteboard, is it accessible to children and are they taught how to use it? This should not just be a resource for use by adults only.			

	In place	Area for development	Comments
Resources for phonics teaching Are there sufficient resources for children? Do the teacher resources include puppets for demonstration, a large clearly visible whiteboard, sticky notes, cards of each phoneme, magnetic letters, and cards for games and activities? Does the practitioner have a well-organised selection of phonics resources to draw on for discrete teaching sessions?			

This list is by no means exhaustive but may give staff a place to start.

References:

Babbling Babies, I CAN Charity.

Brannagan, M. (2015): *Why Language Development is Important to a Child.* Livestrong.com.

Department for children, schools and families (2008): *The Inclusion Development Programme. Supporting children with speech, language and communication needs: Guidance for practitioners in the Early Years Foundation Stage.* The National Strategies Early Years.

Department for Education (2006): *Communication, Language and Literacy Development: audit tool to support improvements in learning and teaching of Communication, Language and Literacy.* Foundationyears.org.uk.

Department for Education (2007): *Supporting children learning English as an additional language: Guidance for practitioners in the Early Years Foundation Stage.* Naldic.org.uk.

National Association for Language Development in the Curriculum

Norman, K. (ed.) (1990, 1992): *Thinking Voices: The Work of the National Oracy Project.* Hodder Education.

Marsh, J. Hallet, E. (eds.) (2008): *Desirable Literacies: approaches to language and literacy in the early years.* SAGE.

Roulstone, S. Law, J. Rush, R. Clegg, J. Peters, T. (2010): *Investigating the role of language in children's early educational outcomes.* Department of Education.

Rvachew, S. (2010): *Language development & Literacy.* Encyclopaedia of Early Childhood Development.

The National Strategies Early Years. (2008): *Every Child a Talker: Guidance for Early Language Lead Practitioners.* Department for children, schools and families.

The National Strategies Early Years. (2008): *Supporting children with speech, language and communication needs: Guidance for practitioners in the Early Years Foundation Stage.* Department for children, schools and families.

Children's mathematical understanding

In 2008 the Department for Education (DfE) published the Williams review, an independent review of mathematics teaching in early years settings and primary schools. The report investigated mathematical development in early years and concluded that mathematics was not taught as successfully as other areas of the curriculum, citing that "opportunities in this area seem to be missed".

The Early Years Foundation Stage (EYFS) annually release data, which confirms that relatively few children meet, or exceed, the required standard in mathematics compared to other areas of the curriculum. Although things have been improving over the last three years, it remains lower than many other early learning goals.

The main barrier to children's mathematical understanding remains the lack of confidence and knowledge held by the adults that work with children. This means that the quality of learning in mathematics is too inconsistent. As outcomes depend on the qualifications and attitudes of the practitioners, it is vital that these adults gain a better understanding of how children develop mathematical concepts and how they might better support all children, with both achievement and progress in mathematics.

What do early years practitioners need to do to address this and ensure that provision for teaching mathematics is appropriate and effective?

1. Create a rich environment to support the development of mathematical understanding

Practitioners need to plan opportunities for children to experience mathematics in everyday routines. Mathematics has to feel real and purposeful to children if they are to really engage with it and see its value.

Practitioners must ensure both indoor and outdoor environments offer opportunities for children to acquire, rehearse and apply their mathematical knowledge. In order to do this, it will be helpful to audit both your indoor and outdoor environment to check that children have a rich and varied menu of experiences in which to engage with, rehearse and acquire early mathematical knowledge and concepts.

Auditing the early years environment to support the teaching of mathematics

This is by no means a comprehensive list but is worth considering as a starter:

Key question	Current position	Next steps
Number: Do you have numbered lines in different places of varying lengths such as 10, 20 and beyond? Are they displayed at a comfortable height for children? Do you give children the opportunity to count real objects regularly, for a real purpose? Do you teach and regularly sing number rhymes and songs? Do they count backwards and forwards?		
Shape & space: Does your outside environment provide a variety of opportunities to experience going through/on top of/under/over/going around/between? Do all adults use this vocabulary and support children in understanding its meaning? Are children regularly given the opportunity to build things, large and small, so that they can experience 3D and 2D shapes? Do adults use the correct vocabulary of shape? Are children encouraged to do the same?		
Measures: Does your setting have real measuring equipment, such as jugs, clocks, timers and measuring tapes, in the play environment? Do adults set up opportunities for children to use the apparatus for realistic reasons? For example, a home corner as a shop or a DIY store. Are children encouraged to record their findings/measurements? Are children able to select tools independently that they want to use to aid any investigation? Do you regularly involve children in cooking activities that require them to measure accurately? Are they encouraged to use the vocabulary of measurement and weight (too much, level, amount, enough etc.)?		
Money: Do you set up a shop in the home corner? Do children have the chance to use real money (sales, visit to the shops)? Do you regularly use the vocabulary of money when talking to children about their everyday experiences?		

Time: Does your routine offer you the opportunity to talk about the pattern of the day/week/year? Do you celebrate birthdays? Do you display and talk about the days of the week and the months of the year? Is there a large clock in all the rooms for the children to see easily? Do you time activities using an egg timer, stopwatch or a countdown timer?		
Sorting & matching: Do you have matching/pairs card games to play? Do you get children matching when they tidy up? Do you have sorting and matching activities outside, such as matching socks on the washing line?		
Pattern: Are threading activities available? Can the children make or copy pattern in various media such as paint, chalk, sand, water and printing? Where **is** maths happening? Where is maths **not** happening?		

2. Offer children the opportunity to learn their maths through play

In all early years settings, play is the natural medium through which children learn. Practitioners need to ensure that they provide the materials, stimulation, encouragement and reason for children to engage in maths play whilst not directing children or interfering. More directed works ceases to be play and becomes adult-led activity. Play is the most effective vehicle through which even the very youngest children begin to develop their understanding of mathematical concepts.

So much of what they do in the beginning requires hands-on, practical experiences that allow children to experiment, research, investigate, observe, practice and discuss. As practitioners, it is crucial that we ensure children have these opportunities planned into the every day. They can respond to particular interests, strengths, seasons of the year and times of the day. We should use their every day experiences to support their maths learning as well as create more artificial experiences that lend themselves to experiencing and learning about discreet maths concepts. Planning for maths learning might include the following most common activities:

- The use of play dough to learn about measurement and shapes, while making comparisons.

- A daily timetable & routines to show the awareness of time.
- An outside area to help learn about prepositions.
- A sand and water area to discuss conservation, volume, shape, pattern, weight.
- Run an imaginative play session to understand sorting and matching through playing shops and homes, for example by setting the table, matching socks from a washing line and role-playing with telephones.
- Physical play activities like threading, to understand pattern and sequence, cars, to understand prepositions, tidying up by sorting by colour or size and playground markings such as a numbered hopscotch to learn patterns.
- The use of books and rhymes is essential, such as Goldilocks where children can learn 'left' to 'right', sequencing and number stories.
- Use nature to understand the concepts of time and measurement, through gardening and planting seeds, and time and pattern, through seasons.

Games and puzzles are also incredibly important in supporting a child's mathematical learning, both pre-number and number. Games such as snap, pairs, old maid, snakes & ladders, jigsaws and lotto all provide excellent opportunities to learn about mathematics. With well-trained and skilful staff, all activities that children engage in can be made into opportunities to learn about maths.

3. Develop mathematical vocabulary

Some children may start at your setting with a good understanding of mathematical words, for others this may be very limited. It is important that practitioners find out the extent of their mathematical vocabulary and the depth of their understanding so that they build on this. When introducing new words, it has to be done in a suitable, practical context, such as with relevant real objects. It is important that adults explain it's meaning many times and use the word regularly over time, referring to new mathematical words only once will do little to promote learning.

Encourage children in context during oral sessions, particularly through your questioning. Using a range of open and closed questions can help identify any misunderstandings children might have so you can address these.

There is a range of mathematical vocabulary that children in early years, at some point, need to be exposed to. Below is a collection of mathematical words that may be used at varying stages of preschool education, before they complete the end of their reception year. Early years practitioners should be familiar with these and know how to use them accurately and understand when it is appropriate to introduce the terms to young children. These include:

Instructions:	**Exploring patterns, shape and space:**	**Position, direction and movement:**
Listen, join in, say Think, imagine, remember Start from, start with, start at Look at, point to, show me Put, place, fit, arrange, rearrange, change, change over, split, separate Carry on, continue, repeat, what comes next? Find, choose, collect Use, make, build Tell me, describe, pick out, talk about, explain, show me Read, write, trace, copy, complete, finish, end Fill in, colour Draw, join (up), ring, count, workout	Shape, pattern, flat, curved, straight, round, Hollow, solid Corner Face, side, edge, end Sort Make, build, draw 3D shapes: cube pyramid, sphere, cone 2D shapes: circle, triangle, square, rectangle, star, diamond Size, bigger, larger, smaller Repeating pattern, match	Over, under, above, below, top, bottom, side, inside, outside, around, in front, behind, front, back, before, after, beside, next to, opposite, apart, between, middle, edge, corner, Left, right, up, down, forwards, backwards, sideways, across, close, far, near, along, through, two, from, towards, away from. Slide, roll, turn, stretch, bend
General	**Calculation**	**Capacity**
Same, different, counters, cubes, blocks, rods Die, dice Dominoes Pegs, pegboard Same way, different way Best way, another way In order, in a different order Not all, every, each	And, add, plus, more Less, take away, fewer, leftover, difference	Full, half full, empty Holds, container
Measures, shape and space		
Measures (general)	**Length**	**Mass**
Measure, size, compare, guess, estimate Enough, not enough, too much, too little Too many, too few Nearly, close to, about the same as Just over, just under	Length, width, height, depth Long, short, tall, high, low Wide, narrow, deep, shallow Thick, thin Longer, shorter, taller, higher, longest, shortest, tallest, highest, etc. Far, near, close	Weigh, weighs, balances Heavy/light Heavier/ lighter Heaviest/ lightest Balance, scales, weight

Time	**Reasoning about numbers or shapes**
Monday, Tuesday and so on, day, week	Pattern
Birthday, holiday	Puzzle
Morning, afternoon, evening, night	Answer
Bedtime, dinnertime, lunchtime, playtime	Right, wrong
Today, yesterday, tomorrow	What could we try next?
Before, after	How did you work it out?
Next, last now, soon, early, late	Count, sort
Quick, quickly, quicker, quickest, quickly	Group, set
Slow, slowly, slower, slowest	Match
Old, older, oldest	Same, different
New, newer, newest	List
Takes longer, takes less time	
Hour, o'clock	
Clock, watch, hands	
Problem-solving involving 'real life' or money	**Comparison and ordering**
Money	Compared
Coin, penny, pence, pound	Double
Price	Half, halve
Cost, buy, sell	Pair
Spend, spent	Count out, share out
Pay	Left, left over
Change	
Dear, costs more	
Cheap, costs less, cheaper	
Costs the same as	
How much…?	
How many…?	
Total	

4. Understand and employ the features of highly effective early years practitioners

- They provide a mathematically stimulating and challenging environment.
- They observe and listen to children to understand their mathematical thinking and develop this systematically.

- They allow children to use their mathematical understanding to solve realistic problems very regularly.
- They discuss children's ideas with them, develop and extend their understanding and use of technically accurate mathematical vocabulary.
- They provide opportunities to practice mathematical skills, to gain confidence and competence in using their new skills.
- They take every opportunity to develop understanding, whether during a teacher-led or child-initiated activity.
- They model mathematical vocabulary during the daily routines and throughout practitioner-led activities.
- They value children's play, talk and mathematical mark-making.
- Through discussion and conversation, they help scaffold children's thinking, introducing new vocabulary and asking open questions to encourage children to talk about their thinking.
- They have a clear understanding of what each child can and cannot do, does and does not know, so that when we introduce new concepts there is no discontinuity, which could lead to misunderstanding for the child.
- They have high expectations of what children can understand and achieve.

It is worth considering, as you interact with your children every day, whether you do the following:

- demonstrate
- model
- explain
- suggest
- provide
- encourage
- ask
- help
- introduce
- comment

5. Distinguish how children's mathematical understanding develops

All children will learn about mathematics by following three stages:

Concrete:

- They use and hold items and resources whilst learning about mathematical concepts. They learn through doing.
- Children use apparatus and learn their mathematics through a hands-on experience.
- For example, in order to solve the problem of "what is five plus two?", they would need to take five objects and count them, take two objects and count them, physically put them altogether and then count all that they have again.

Pictorial:

- Based on the practical experience they have had, they no longer need to 'do'. They are able to draw pictures to represent what they had previously physically done themselves.
- At this level, children will no longer need to physically manipulate objects to solve problems. They are able to visualise the problem and record it using pictures.
- For example, in order to solve the problem of "what is five plus two?" they might draw five apples then draw two apples and then count how many they have drawn altogether. Very young children will record their findings in their own way, which may not be easily understood by others, but this is to be encouraged.

Symbolic:

- Children are able to swap their own individual pictorial representations for universally accepted symbols such as +,-.x,£ and numbers. This is a far step from the practical experience they began with. They are only able to use these symbols successfully because they had a comprehensive practical experience when they were younger or less experienced.
- For example, in order to solve the problem of "what is five plus two?" they are able to record: 5+2= and complete the problem mentally or using a number line.

When any new mathematical concept is introduced to children, it is crucial that practitioners start with the concrete stage before moving to the pictorial stage and finally use symbols at the symbolic stage. In early years settings, most of your work typically will be in the concrete stage.

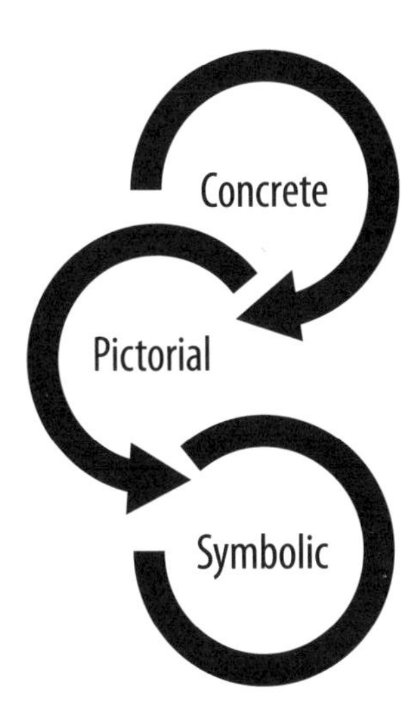

The mistake that too many practitioners make is to move from the concrete stage to the pictorial stage too quickly and from the pictorial stage to the symbolic stage too quickly. For the most part of children's early years experience, they will be working almost entirely within the concrete, using real apparatus to help them develop an understanding of mathematics.

At the start of children's learning, the balance between concrete, pictorial and symbolic should be as follows:

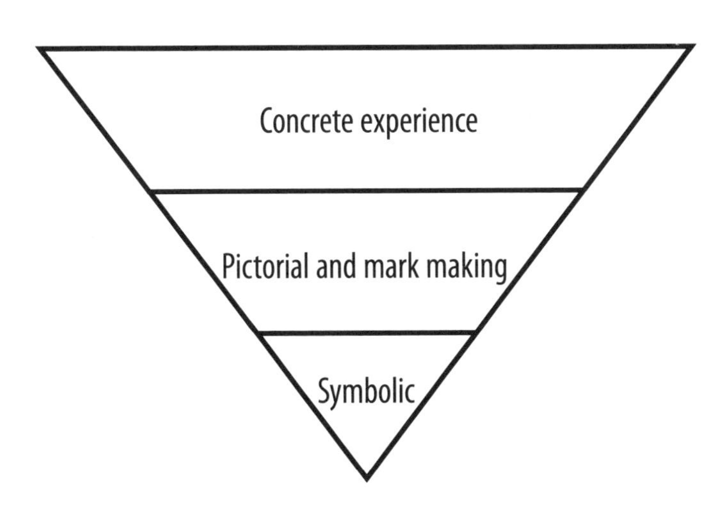

Young children should spend the greatest amount of their time at the concrete stage with hands-on experiences that offer meaning to them. There is often a tendency to move away from the concrete experiences and get children recording and using symbols too quickly. This stores up problems for the future because, although they may learn the tricks to use when recording work symbolically, they will not understand their meaning or purpose. If they miss out on the necessary practical foundations, they will have a problem in understanding mathematics later on in their education.

Numbers and counting

Learning about numbers is the most difficult challenge for both adults and children because children need to learn that an abstract symbol, such as 1, 2 and 3, represents a specific amount or quantity. They must also understand that this applies universally, no matter what it is that they are counting, whether it is a tiny pebble or a huge bus.

This is called number conservation. Children need to understand the 'three-ness' of three, the 'eight-ness' of eight. They also need to understand the value of these symbols, such as that four is less than seven but more than two.

Start by introducing numbers one to five and then six to ten. After this, any larger number being based on the same number system is more familiar for them. Children need as many experiences, physical, visual and oral, to begin to understand the concept. It is important that adults provide almost endless opportunities to talk about and experience numbers, both in terms of real day-to-day objects and numerical symbols.

Children's understanding can be developed in the following ways:

- Count out loud with children every day, both forwards and backwards.
- Compare numbers regularly.
- Get children to count reliably every day, it is a habit they need to get into as accuracy is essential to be successful in maths.
- Model to children how to order into groups to count more accurately, such as four sets of two to make eight. Model to the children touching each object as you count so that children learn the relationship between each object and counting up.
- Talk to children about numbers in everyday experience. Help them to see that maths is all around them and can be found in everything they do.
- Have number lines that children can hop along to as they count, both forwards and backwards.
- Have number games to play such as dominoes, snakes and ladders and anything that can involve a dice.

- Read and sing stories and rhymes that have a number theme.
- Have number charts around the room that are at a child's height.
- Have magnetic and foam numbers for children to play with. Make sure you have numbers in the outdoor environment too. Have some displayed but also have loose numbers that children can physically pick up and arrange in the correct order.
- Show children how to write down the symbol for numbers as you count them together.

The secret of mastering number conservation and understanding the number system is to ensure children observe, rehearse and experiment with number in a variety of different ways, many times a day and in different contexts whilst using different resources. It must always be done with great meaning and purpose.

References:

All Party Parliamentary Group for Maths & Numeracy (2015): *Maths and numeracy in the early years.* Nationalnumeracy.org.uk.

Bennett, E. (2011): *Making it count: The crucial role of the practitioner in promoting mathematical learning in the EYs.* The National Strategies Early Years.

Department for children, schools and families (2011): *Children thinking mathematically: PRSN essential knowledge for Early Years practitioners.* Foundationyears.org.uk.

Department for children, schools and families (2008): *Review of Mathematics Teaching in Early Years Settings and Primary Schools – Interim Report from Sir Peter Williams.* Education.gov.uk.

Donald, B. (2011): *Mathematics in the Early Years: How can we provide effective support to develop children's concepts for learning in mathematics in partnership with their parents?*

Gifford, S. (2015): Early Years Mathematics: *How to Create a Nation of Mathematics Lovers?* NRICH: Enriching Mathematics.

Learning through Landscapes (2008): *Open Up to Outdoor Mathematics: Supporting children's developing problem solving reasoning and numeracy skills through good use of natural and man made materials in the outdoor environment.*

Palacios, R. (2014): *Helping Children Make Sense of Numbers: Number Sense.* The Huffington Post.

Stanberry, K. *Preschool Math Grows Up: Tips for Teacher.* Getreadytoread.org.How children learn maths: A,C,Buris 2010

Outdoor provision

Over the years, we have seen a decline in the opportunities for young children to play in the outdoor environment. Many more families live in flats with no access to a garden, parents are more anxious about allowing their children outside unless very closely supervised and technology has seduced both parents and children into believing that it provides a comprehensive entertainment and learning platform. Opportunities to play and learn outside provide a crucial element to the healthy development of all children. If you are not convinced of the importance of outdoor provision, ask any adult to think back to their childhood and recall their most exciting and memorable play experience. Chances are they will tell you about something they did outside.

We know that children benefit hugely from playing outside and learning from nature. Our curriculum places high importance on ensuring that settings offer children a daily opportunity to play and learn outside. A quality, well-used outdoor environment will make or break any Ofsted judgement. That is not to say that schools need to invest vast sums of money or that settings need to have expansive areas to use. Some of the very best outdoor environments I have seen are in urban areas where space is limited and money tight but the imagination and determination of staff abounds.

At Netherfield Primary School in Nottingham, the early years leader describes the outdoor environment as "mirroring the indoor environment as much as possible so that children have access to all of the same kinds of activities and learning opportunities outside as they would inside." We know that some children prefer to learn outside rather than indoors and would miss out if the areas were too dissimilar. It is certainly worth considering whether the outdoor area is as stimulating and interesting as that which you have provided inside.

What does high quality outdoor provision look like?

Activities and resources available to children need to offer rich learning and investigative opportunities that are different from those they may experience at home. They need to be more ambitious and messier, perhaps on a larger scale and in this way they will be irresistible to children. Outdoor activities need to create a sense of joy and excitement that will sustain a child's interest over a prolonged period.

The activities prepared must respond to the needs of children, which can be achieved by being thoroughly assessed by staff members. For example, those with poorly developed gross motor skills need to be able to rehearse and refine these skills outside. Those who struggle to develop social skills need to be directed to those activities that require negotiation, sharing and teamwork. Areas of focus will change as children's needs do.

The staff members must understand that it is the **experiences** that children are exposed to which are important rather than the equipment that the setting provides. The most highly effective provision does not rely on spending a great deal of money. If the staff members make the most of what they have available to them, are enthusiastic and positive, then they will create meaningful learning experiences for young children.

At different times, the outdoor environment needs to provide opportunities for children to develop skills in all areas of learning. Have you made the right provisions for physical development, language and communication, mathematical development, science, art, music and social skills? There should be comprehensive coverage of all areas of learning, which are thoroughly planned to meet a child's needs.

It is also important that the outdoor provisions should not remain the same at all times. Obviously the large apparatus will remain static but in other ways it needs to be organic, to change and develop over time. Staff members need to introduce new and different things regularly that respond to the seasons, weather and the themes that children are developing and learning in class. It may be useful to create weather boxes that come out for use when it is windy (such as kites and wind chimes), sunny (which can include water play, mirrors and beach items), snowy (spades, moulds, boots & tyres for printing) or rainy (umbrellas, wellies, containers, wet weather gear).

It is a good idea to consider creating an outdoor calendar that identifies outdoor learning opportunities for the whole school year. Adding these to your curriculum map will enhance a child's experiences and learning, ensuring that they are regularly exposed to the outdoors regardless what the weather or season is.

Whilst apparatus and resources are crucial, it is also important that settings make opportunities for the outdoor environment to be rich in language and number too. The best settings have number lines displayed, have phonics (graphemes, phonemes, digraphs etc.) and key vocabulary displayed. You can utilise these in a number of way, for example get the children to line up in order next to the numbered apparatus at the end of the outside play session. It is also good idea to have prepositions around the climbing frame and specific words around the water and sand for children to apply and use. Children need to see language and numbers everywhere. Settings are usually very good at providing such stimulation indoors and in class but many fail to extend this to the outdoor environment.

The settings must also allow for an element of risk so that children can learn to be aware of risk and how to manage it. The planned activities should be open-ended and investigative, allowing children to access them at their own level. Differentiation is achieved through the skilled interaction with staff that support, encourage and extend children's learning both in adult-led and child-initiated activities.

It is also important that children have experience of the four elements:

Earth	This includes direct contact with different types of soil, sand, mud and clay. Do they have the opportunity to dig, mix, build and sculpt? Are there different types of stone for them to feel and climb over? Do they grow and care for plants?
Water	Access to an outdoor water supply is vital for learning. Children need to use pumps, waterwheels, pipes and containers. They can make boats, rafts and dams and pour water to make puddles and streams as well as water the plants.
Air	Watch the wind at work with flags, wind chimes, feathers, washing lines, ribbons, leaves. They also can make bubbles. They can listen to the wind, watch windmills and fly kites. They can watch and investigate birds and insects in flight.
Fire	Investigate the sun by looking at shadows at different times of the day. Have a sundial, mirrors to reflect light and look through coloured filters. If staff members are Forest School trained then they can set up a campfire area, obviously this would need to be very carefully supervised.

How do you create this at your setting?

It is important that all staff regularly review the use and effectiveness of the outdoor areas. Although the EYFS leader may run a review session, it is crucial that all the staff are involved with the process of evaluation and planning. When people feel involved and know their ideas are listened to and acted upon, they will work hard to ensure the learning spaces outdoors work well.

All staff must get to know the 'Early Learning Goals' very well and regularly refer to these when planning for the outside. Unless staff have a very good understanding of required stages of development in each area of learning, they cannot know what to provide in order for children to practice and acquire the necessary skills and develop understanding.

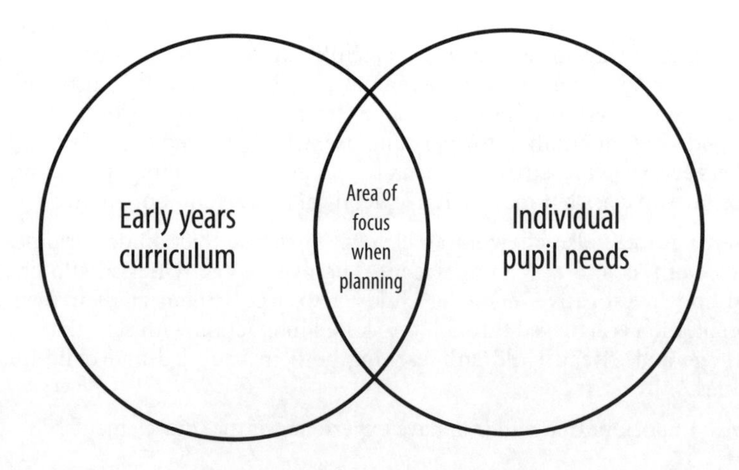

In highly effective settings, staff are regularly involved in a cycle of notice, assess and respond for individual pupils. Through regular observation, assessment of individual children and armed with a secure knowledge of the early learning goals, staff can ensure that children's needs are met and learning opportunities are pitched correctly for the child's ability and stage of development. Planning needs to focus on the overlap between the content of early years curriculum and the needs of the individual. Please refer to the diagram on the adjacent page.

The creation of high quality outdoor environments relies heavily on the creativity and enthusiasm of the staff involved. They need to come up with an armoury of activities and resources that will:

- Stimulate children
- Create awe and wonder
- Offer opportunities for imaginative play and interaction with others
- Give children first hand experiences
- Allow children to experience joy, fascination and curiosity through exploration
- Help children make sense of their world

These ideas will come from experience and research and I cannot emphasise enough how important it is that staff have the opportunity to visit settings of excellence that will inspire them and give them an understanding of what excellent practice looks like. It can be some of the most valuable professional development staff will ever experience.

Planning to develop your outside learning space

Planning for improvement involves four stages:

Involving all staff, children and the wider community will be crucial to success.

Any changes to make will need to be sustainable and manageable. For instance, whilst establishing willow domes or mazes might seem like a fabulous learning opportunity for children in your care, they require a great deal of maintenance throughout the year. You will need to make sure that you have the staff who are available and committed enough to commit to the additional effort required to maintain such installations.

Given the fact that the quality of the outdoor learning experience needs to be as rich and varied as that which the children receive indoors, it would seem sensible to check that your outdoor environment allows children to develop in all areas of the early years curriculum. It may be useful to complete the following audit:

Area of learning and development:	Aspect	How our outdoor environment encourages development in this aspect:
Physical development	Moving and handling	
	Health and self-care	
Understanding the world	People and communities	
	The world technology	
Mathematics	Numbers	
	Shape, space and measures	
Communication and language	Listening and attention	
	Understanding	
	Speaking	
Literacy	Reading	
	Writing	
Personal, social and emotional development	Making relationships, self-confidence and self-awareness	
	Managing feelings and behaviour	
Expressive arts and design	Exploring and using media and materials	
	Being imaginative	

It may be useful to ask the following questions:

- Are there any aspects of learning and development that your current outdoor learning environment does not support?
- What improvements do you need to make to your outdoor environment to ensure that all aspects of the curriculum are adequately covered?
- If you are not sure what you could do to improve your outdoor learning environment, where can you go for support? This could include your local authority, websites and visits to provisions that you know have been judged as outstanding.

- Who is going to maintain the outdoor environment? What time of year will this need to be done? How frequently? Has this been planned for?

Although no two outdoor learning environments will ever be the same, there are certain key features which all settings should include. They are:

- The outdoor area is secure and access is monitored carefully so that children can move freely between the indoor and outdoor environments.
- Children should have both shade and shelter so that they can work outdoors all year round.
- Appropriate clothing must be available so that children can work outdoors all year round such as summer hats, Wellington boots, waterproof clothing, hats and gloves. There should be drying facilities and a washing machine within the setting.
- Storage must be appropriate; it is safe and children can access resources and put them away independently.
- There should be an electrical and a water supply that allows for extended outdoor learning.
- The interface between indoor and outdoor must have an easily cleaned floor surface that is non-slip.

If you are going to grow fruit and vegetables with the children, it is worth carefully planning this. The Royal Horticultural Society have offered a useful annual planner:

Autumn Term		Spring term		Summer term	
Sow/Plant	**Harvest**	**Sow/Plant**	**Harvest**	**Sow/Plant**	**Harvest**
Broad beans Peas Strawberries Raspberries Lettuce Garlic Wheat Apples Pears Blueberries Blackberries (thornless)	Raspberries Pumpkins Courgettes Runner beans Sweetcorn Tomatoes Carrots Parsnips Leaks Main crop Potatoes Spinach Apples Pears Blackberries (thornless) Wheat	Peas Broad beans Potatoes Radish Lettuce Parsnips Leaks Spring onion Herbs Spinach Wheat Carrots	Lettuce Leeks Parsnips	Lettuce Runner beans Courgettes Cucumber French beans pumpkins Radish Sweetcorn Tomatoes Carrots Spring onion Main crop Potatoes	Broad beans, Peas Potatoes French beans Strawberries Blueberries, Sweetcorn Runner beans Cucumber Courgette Lettuce Radish Garlic Onions Carrots Spinach Spring onions
Other jobs		**Other jobs**		**Other jobs**	
Dig soil		Fork in compost		Sow tender crops inside in April	
Mulch bare soil		Rake		Plant out tender crops in May	
Plan garden		Warm soil for early growing		Protect crops from pests weed	
Plan fruit		Protect early sowings from frost		Water	
Order seeds		Sow hardy crops		Mulch around plants	

Off-site activities

At times, you may decide that you need to take the children off-site for outdoor learning experiences. If this facility is easily available to you, it can significantly enhance the experience of the children in your care. However, it is absolutely crucial that such activities are carefully planned and that the children's safety is paramount. Before taking the children off-site it is important to consider the following:

- Have you consulted all policies and procedures for the setting and complied with them?
- Does your insurance policy cover the activity you have planned? If you are visiting a site owned by another body, do they have public liability insurance?

- Have you informed parents and sought their permission?
- Has a staff member completed a risk assessment and have senior leaders agreed the visit?
- Is the adult to child ratio appropriate?
- Have all the staff members and children attending the activity been well briefed, do they understand expectations in terms of behaviour and what to do in the event of an emergency?
- Is there provision to cater for first aid needs such as a paediatric first aider and first-aid equipment?
- Do you have all the staff members and children's emergency contact details?
- Will the children be anywhere close to roads and do all staff members on the trip understand the road safety procedures?
- Do any children have medical needs that require medication to come with them, such as an inhaler?
- Do staff members have the facility to communicate both with the setting and with other staff members who are off-site?
- Are there facilities for children to toilet and wash their hands?

How do you make sure outdoor provision is used effectively?

All staff members need to be committed to ensuring year round 'free flow' for children. This commitment needs to be further strengthened by a clear and unequivocal school policy statement. It is very easy, especially in cold or wet weather, to keep the door to the outside shut. Staff may have the very best protective intentions, not wishing children to become too cold or wet. However, if they are carefully supervised and properly dressed then children can and should be outdoors every day for some period of time beyond the usual break and lunchtimes.

It is important to ensure that all those involved in educating early years understand that the outdoor environment is not an attractive 'add-on' but rather an essential part of children's daily learning experience. It needs to be planned for, used and regularly reviewed to ensure that provision is highly effective in helping children develop and learn.

References:

Bilton, H. (2010): *Outdoor Learning in the Early Years: Management and Innovation.* David Fulton Publishers.

Council for Learning Outside the Classroom. (2009): *Benefits for Early Years Learning Outside the Classroom.* Lotc.org.uk.

Department for Education (2012): *Development Matters in the Early Years Foundation Stage.* Foundationyears.org.uk.

Norfolk County Council (2009): *Early Years Outdoor Learning: A Toolkit for Developing Early Years Outdoor Provision.* Schools.norfolk.gov.uk.

Ofsted. (2015): *Using the physical environment as a tool for teaching: Netherfield Primary School. Gov.uk.*

Outdoor Matters! (2007): *Effective Practice: Outdoor Learning.* Early Years Foundation Stage.

Robertson, J. (2014): *Dirty Teaching: A Beginner's Guide to Learning Outdoors.* Independent Thinking Press. s

Safeguarding children

The Department for Education defines safeguarding as being concerned with:

- Protecting children from maltreatment.
- Preventing impairment of children's health or development.
- Ensuring that the children are growing up in circumstances consistent with the provision of safe and effective care.
- Taking action to enable all children to have the best outcomes.

In this chapter, I will discuss particular areas of responsibility and focus that all early years settings should consider. It is perhaps easiest to consider safeguarding in the sections highlighted in this chapter.

The child

Some of the questions you can ask yourself are:

- If the child was at a previous setting, are there any notes or concerns raised in previous records that you need to be aware of?
- If you completed a home visit, were there any concerns raised at this point?
- Do the children feel safe? How do you know? Who do you ask about this? You should be consulting children, even very young ones, as well as their parents and carers.
- Many small children will lack the language skills to talk about this, so a useful exercise is to give children a camera and asked them to take pictures of areas of the setting where they feel safe and areas of the setting where they do not.
- This will provide excellent information for leaders and managers to understand any necessary improvements they need to make to their environment.

The staff

In regards to the safety of the children on a day-to-day basis, it is crucial that somebody within your setting or organisation is taking responsibility for ensuring that:

- The staff members employed at the school have all been cleared to work with young children.
- All staff interview panels include at least one staff member who has completed the 'safer recruitment' training.
- A single central record is kept of all staff working at the setting which includes the following information:

Name, including their surname and forename
Job title(s)
Address in the form of a full postal address and including a postcode
Their date of birth
The date the person joined the school
The date the person took up this role
A copy of their QTS/Professional Qualifications with the date it was checked and by whom
Barring list – method/date checked and by whom
A DBS check including the date of certificate and disclosure reference number
An overseas police checks with a date specifying when it was checked and by whom
A prohibition from teaching check, through Secure Access
Childcare (Disqualification) Regulations 2009 declaration
Right to work in the UK with evidence seen, the date it was seen and by whom
Their proof of identity, which is often covered by documentation seen for the DBS check
For supply teachers, a confirmation note from agency that checks have been completed

This single central record must be regularly updated and no sections of it must be left incomplete. If there is some delay in obtaining information required, say if perhaps the staff member is coming from overseas, then to ensure that no child is at risk a senior member of staff or leader must complete the assessment. This may include prohibiting staff from working on a one-to-one basis unsupervised with children until the correct paperwork has been obtained and checked.

As well as the points made above, a register must be kept to show what safeguarding training all staff members have completed and the date it was completed. This training needs to be regularly updated, at least once every three years. For designated officers, the training is more regular. All staff, including those who may not come into contact with children, must complete basic level one in safeguarding training. This needs to be done as soon as possible after their appointment.

If face-to-face training is not immediately available, online training can be organised instead. Staff should be provided with a certificate to demonstrate completion of training and a copy of this must be filed, along with the date of completion. There should be no member of staff who has not completed the training or whose training is out of date. It would be sensible for the staff member who looks after the single central record to also look after the safeguarding training register. It would be prudent that all staff also have an understanding of the 'Prevent' agenda and have had some basic training about this.

The designated officer must have completed the appropriate training and this must be updated every two years. Designated safeguarding officers also should complete 'Prevent' training. Local authorities will have a list of training that they can offer throughout the year. Designated officers should look at this to meet their needs and that of all staff within the setting.

All staff members should be very clear about what to do if they have a concern about a child. They need to know how to record their concerns, what format they should use and whom this information should be reported to. All settings should have a whistleblowing policy and staff should know how to raise concerns and with whom if they are worried about the behaviour of any staff members. All staff are effectively inducted when they start work at the setting and part of the induction programme includes discussions about safeguarding, staff behaviour and staff protocols.

A question to ask is whether, apart from key workers, can children identify trusted adult with whom they could communicate about any concerns?

Paperwork: compliance and record keeping

There are two key documents that staff must be very familiar with. These are:

- The Department for Education's (DfE) statutory guidance to schools 'Keeping children safe in education', which came into force in April 2014 and was updated in March 2015. It sets out the responsibilities placed on schools to safeguard and promote the welfare of children.
- The statutory guidance 'Working together to safeguard children' which provides two organisations and professionals who provide services to children. This guidance was updated in March 2015.

These two are so important, that it is worth getting staff to sign and date a register to demonstrate they have read at least the executive summaries. Both documents are due an update so ensure that your designated officer is aware of when these become available via the Department for Education and respond to any changes accordingly.

In addition to these documents, designated safeguarding officers must also be familiar with the following:

- Prevent duty guidance for England and Wales, the duty of schools and other providers with regard to preventing people from being drawn into terrorism.
- The statutory framework for the early years foundation stage. Setting the standards for learning, development and care for children from birth to age five (DfE, 2014).
- Disqualification under the Childcare Act 2006. Statutory guidance for local authorities, maintained schools, independent schools, academies and free schools (DfE, 2015).

All of the above publications are available from either the Ofsted or the gov.uk website.

The first two documents identified are excellent places to start when considering how effective safeguarding practice and procedures are in your own setting and in helping you to identify what works well in your setting and what needs to be improved. It may be useful to use the two documents to review practice at your setting in the following way:

Safeguarding Children:

A response to guidance in 'Keeping children safe in education' & 'Working together to safeguard children'.

Key Issue	Current Position	Next Step
There is a designated safeguarding lead.		
Setting has a responsibility to identify children who may be in need of extra help or who are suffering, or are likely to suffer, significant harm.		
All staff members should be aware of systems within their school which support safeguarding and these should be explained to them as part of staff induction.		
All staff members should also receive appropriate child protection training, which is regularly updated.		
All school staff members should be aware of the signs of abuse and neglect.		
A child who goes missing from education is a potential indicator of abuse or neglect.		
Governing bodies must ensure that they comply with their duties under legislation. They must ensure that the policies, procedures and training in their schools are effective and comply with the law at all times.		
Governing bodies should ensure that the school contributes to inter-agency working.		
Governing bodies should ensure that their safeguarding arrangements take into account the procedures and practice of the local authority as part of the inter-agency safeguarding procedures.		
Usually the chair is nominated to liaise with the local authority and/or partner agencies on issues of child protection and in the event of allegations of abuse made against the headteacher.		
Governing bodies should ensure there is an effective child protection policy in place together with a staff behaviour policy or code of conduct.		

The designated safeguarding lead officer should undergo updated child protection training every two years. The headteacher and all staff members should undergo child protection training, which is updated regularly in line with advice from the Local Safeguarding Children Board.		
Governing bodies should consider how children may be taught about safeguarding, including online.		
Procedures must be in place to handle allegations against members of staff and volunteers.		
Governing bodies must appoint a designated teacher to promote the educational achievement of children who are looked after and to ensure that this person has appropriate training.		
DBS checks are required.		
An offer of appointment must be conditional upon satisfactory completion of pre-employment checks.		
A DBS certificate must be obtained from the candidate, before or as soon as practicable after appointment. Alternatively, if the applicant has subscribed to it and gives permission, the school may undertake an online update check through the DBS Update Service.		
Schools and colleges must keep a single central record.		
Under no circumstances should a volunteer, in respect of whom no checks have been obtained, be left unsupervised or allowed to work in regulated activity.		
Providing early help is more effective in promoting the welfare of children than reacting later.		
Effective sharing of information between professionals and local agencies is essential.		
The timeliness of an assessment is a critical element of the quality of that assessment and the outcomes for the child.		

Recording concerns and information

How a setting records information and concerns, and how they store these records, is absolutely crucial.

All staff should have a means through which they can record any concerns or observations regarding safeguarding. Most settings will have a booklet of pro forma so that it can be completed by staff and handed to the designated officer. They might look like this:

Child Protection Record

Body Map(for mapping any injury)

Date: **Name of Child:** **D.O.B.**

Form completed by:

Front	**Back**

Notes:

Name of Child:	DOB:	Date of incident/disclosure:
Reported by:		
Details: What? Who does it involve? When? Where?		
Action taken by Designated Officer:		

The designated officer should keep a careful record of any conversations that they have had with children's services or other services that the child or family might be involved with regarding concerns about a child. In addition to recording the content of the conversation, make a note of agreed actions both by the school and other agencies. Always take a note of the name of the person you are dealing with, the time and the date of the conversation or telephone call. These notes can then be photocopied and put in individual children's safeguarding files, as appropriate.

The best practice would be to have your safeguarding files for individual children at the setting 'RAG rated' as follows:

Red files mean there is active and current involvement with children's services.

Amber files mean that there is some concern about a child although not serious enough to meet a threshold for involving children services. Often these files are gathering evidence before a referral is made.

Green file mean that there have been previous concerns or involvement with children's services, but not currently a concern. These files are kept as historical evidence and can be referred to in future if necessary to offer background and context.

Red, amber and green plastic folders or envelopes are easy and cheap to acquire from any stationery shop.

At the end of each academic year the designated officer, as part of a report to the governing body or senior managers, should anonymously report all cases referred to children's services in that academic year and their outcomes. It is important for governors to have an understanding of the number of cases that the school is dealing with, they also need to be reassured that each case has been dealt with appropriately and that children are safe. The following is a possible format you may wish to use:

Name of Setting – Child Protection Referral Outcomes: Academic Year 20xx-xx

(Example)

Name of Child/Children *(Anonomised for Governors)*	**Referral date**	**Outcome**	**Next steps for school**
AB *(Example)*	15.04.2016	Family worker in place Involvement of EWO- attendance panel set for xx.xx.xx Children's Services closed case May 20xx.	Carefully monitor attendance & punctuality Ensure agreed actions happen after meetings 6 weekly attendance figures to designated officer. Family worker continues to work with family. Ensure next teacher knows to look out & alert staff re any attendance issues.
CD			
EF			
Number of Safeguarding meetings held this academic year to discuss a child or family associated with this setting:		**Number of meetings held that had representation from a knowledgeable staff member of the setting:**	

Common features of excellent Safeguarding Practice:

- All staff have completed their training and all is up to date. All staff know who the Designated Officer is and that any concerns should be reported to them.
- Designated Officers keeps very careful records of events, people involved and agreed actions. They create a chronological paper trail that is easy to understand.
- All staff ,including the Designated officer, act in a timely manner and in the very best interests of the children.
- The setting has careful policies designed to protect both children and staff. These policies are adhered to by all staff. Policies and practice are reviewed annually and any regional or national recommendations are acted upon.
- When a meeting is called to discuss a child or a family, a knowledgeable representative from the setting is always present.
- The setting has a very clear policy regarding Safer Recruitment which is adhered to for all appointments to the school.
- Staff are clear about the use of technology with children, staff and their parents. There is an Acceptable Use policy which is up to date ,fit for purpose and adhered to by all.

Ref: inspecting safeguarding in early years, education and skills

References:

Department for Education. (2015): *Working together to safeguard children.* Gov.uk.

Ofsted. (2016): *Inspecting safeguarding in early years, education and skills settings: Guidance for inspectors undertaking inspection under the common inspection framework.* Gov.uk.

Behaviour management

When 30 children walk through the doors into your classroom at the start of the new academic year, they will be 30 children who all have, to a lesser or greater extent, a different understanding of what it is to behave. Some will have had their behaviour managed in a highly effective way at home, with high standards set for them. Others may be used to ignoring what an adult tells them to do in the full knowledge that sooner or later that adult will give up trying to persuade the child to do as they are told. These children see requests to behave as a negotiation, a war of attrition that they are likely to win if they just keep disregarding the instructions.

In more extreme cases, you may have children in your class who have never been set expectations regarding their behaviour. Their parents have rarely told the child 'no' or intervened if they have been doing or saying something unacceptable. When such children are faced with a more disciplinary approach they often have disproportionately dramatic reactions. They have developed a heightened sense of self-importance and really struggle with doing anything they do not want to.

Regardless of any child's starting point, for those adults managing them in the classroom, the most important thing is to have in mind a very clear understanding of what acceptable behaviour is and what it looks like in the classroom. This understanding has to be shared and agreed amongst all the adults who work together because a consistent approach for children will be the key to effective behaviour management.

The importance of routine

Children thrive on routine. They need to know that each school day has a pattern to it. They take comfort in the predictability of their days and become unsettled and possibly distressed when they are faced with too much change. It is important therefore that classroom routines are firmly established at the start of each new academic year and that these are adhered to throughout. To begin with, it may be helpful to have a pictorial representation of each day. Children can easily understand such a model and it can be used to show them what happens next; in this way nothing is a surprise to them.

Apart from timetabling routines, children also benefit from a consistent approach being employed by all those adults who they come into contact with whether that is in the classroom, the dining room or the playground. In the best practice, children receive the same message from any adult that they communicate with regarding behavioural expectations or school routines. As managers, it is crucial that we invest time in revisiting these regularly with our established staff, as well as ensuring any induction programme highlights the importance of consistency to all new members of staff.

Positive behaviour management

Almost all children are desperate to please. Once they have developed a relationship with you, they will seek your approval and will do almost anything to get it. Children also respond best to being praised rather than criticised and, as a practitioner, it is far more satisfying to focus on what children are doing right than on what they are getting wrong. Praise and reward are the two most useful weapons in your behaviour management armoury.

Praise: children love to be noticed, especially if this is public and in front of their peers. Never underestimate the power of praise. Even with the most challenging child, adults will be able to find things to praise them for.

Reward: this can involve sticker charts, star charts, choosing a favourite toy, choosing a friend to play with, being chosen to do something and being given extra time with an activity they love. All of these are highly effective at moderating poor behaviour.

Disapproval: this often proves to be far more effective than raising your voice. Shouting at a child is poor practice, unless they are in immediate danger of harming themselves or others, and shows a lack of control and professionalism from the adult. It is more effective to explain that you are disappointed. It is important that we help children to cultivate a conscience. Feeling slightly guilty for a short amount of time is an essential part of children learning the difference between right and wrong. Remember that this is only for a very short period of time, a couple of minutes at the most. Children have to know that they are forgiven and can make a fresh start without an adult holding any sort of grudge or reminding them constantly what they did wrong.

Do not expect too much from children too quickly, do not set targets that they cannot achieve or expectations that they cannot meet or you will both be left disappointed. When first working with children or when introducing a new behaviour expectation, it might be useful to explain to children why they need to conform to your expectation. Do not give elaborate explanations why you expect certain behaviours, but if children understand there are simple reasons for your rules then they are more likely to comply. For example, informing children that we have to put the toys away at the end of the day because otherwise we might not be able to find them tomorrow.

It may be useful to plot all the members of your class on a behaviour continuum to ensure all staff members know about any potential difficulties and to identify the best approach to take in order to modify or improve behaviour.

Extremely well behaved	Occasional outbursts of poor behaviour	Very poor behaviour
Where would you plot the children in your class?		
←		
Very biddable. Listens to adults and responds accordingly. Can be trusted to behave/be kind to others/play safely. Understands and conforms to social norms in terms of how to speak to and interact with both children and adults. Behaviour is easily managed by adults through non-verbal cues, for example a facial expression of disapproval. Child is extremely keen to secure approval from adults.	Child usually does as they are asked, although sometimes this may take more than one request. Behaviour deteriorates if child is tired or immediately after an extended period of time at home, for example a holiday. They recognise what is expected of them in school and want to conform but at times, it can be an effort.	Does not listen to adults or respect their authority. Appears to have no boundaries and cannot be trusted to be on their own with some equipment or to play with children without some incident. Does not conform to social norms, for example they shout at children and adults, hits or pushes other children/adults, easily prone to tears.
Name:	Name:	Name:

Sometimes you will encounter children who demonstrate controlling behaviour, for example they have to be in charge at all times when playing or engaging with others. How do you help them to move away from this need to be in control? Adults need to plan plenty of daily, short and sharp activities where the child is not in control; they have to follow the lead and instructions of somebody else. To begin with, it will require adult supervision to ensure that the child does not dominate.

Eventually children will begin to get the picture of what acceptable behaviour looks like once they have had behaviour modelled, interventions from an adult each time a child attempts to dominate and praise when they allow others to take the lead.

What about pupils who demonstrate characteristics of being a victim? What can you do to support them so that they stop seeing themselves as a victim?

Usually such children are lacking in confidence and self-esteem, so it is important to focus on building this. For such children, think about what it is they are particularly good at, for example are they knowledgeable about a particular subject? When you have identified these strengths, plan opportunities for children to demonstrate these and share their knowledge with their peers. If you are planning such an activity though, ensure that you have created a safe environment in which they will feel comfortable and succeed. At the same time, they will need to learn to develop and apply strategies to deal with more domineering children. These can be modelled to children in the first instance, through role-play, which offers a safe environment to practice being assertive.

When you are faced with a child whose behaviour is proving particularly challenging and hard to manage, an individual plan will be advisable. It will help you identify exactly what the problem is, how to address it and to ensure that all staff employ a consistent approach.

Behaviour Support Plan		
Child's name:	Date of plan:	Review date:
Behaviour to reduce:		
Prevention: Staff will…	If an incident occurs: Staff will…	
Parent/Guardian views:	Date agreed: Signed: Parent/carer: ________ Practitioner: ________	

The role of early years practitioners, and in particular key workers, is absolutely vital in supporting children to learn how to behave appropriately in school. There are some obvious considerations that will ensure children have the best chance of developing behaviours that are appropriate to their school lives.

The environment

You must ask yourself:

- Does the curriculum you plan stimulate children's interest?
- Is there enough for them to do?

If your plan for children is not engaging and does not foster their curiosity, they are less likely to be engaged and will quickly lose interest. This can lead to a decline in behaviour.

Given that the majority of very young children do not have the language required to express themselves, we have to ensure that our curriculum allows them to express themselves in other ways for example through movement, mark-making, modelling, story and song.

Do we have enough high quality resources for all the children we serve? Of course children have to learn to take turn and share but many frustrations can be avoided and disputes minimised if we have enough materials for all children to use.

Do we give children enough opportunity for physical exercise? Some children need to be able to go outside and run off their energy before being expected to concentrate for long periods of time on something more technical or challenging. If you know your class well enough, you will know which children this might apply to.

Links with parents

Parents are not always aware that their children may display behaviours that are not acceptable outside their family. It takes very sensitive handling to give parents bad news about their child, particularly as you might be the first adult to say anything negative about their child. Regardless, it is important that parents do know about any potential problems early on so that together you can work to address them. It helps if you ensure the following:

- It is a private matter; never talk to parents about their children within earshot of other parents.
- If you are feeling cross with a child, make sure you have calmed down before you see the parent. Being emotional or heated will not help anybody.
- Make sure you have notes and evidence that will support what you are saying to parents.
- Sound optimistic, for example 'I'm sure this is just a little blip, however...'
- Try not to just concentrate on the negative, ensure that parents are also told when their children behave well.
- Make sure you record your meeting, with notes about what you said, what the parent said and what you have both agreed to do moving forward.

As a practitioner, if you feel that behaviour management remains an issue, it is worth spending time reflecting on your current practice to check that the adults and setting offer everything possible to ensure children behave well.

Behaviour management audit

	All the time	Most of the time	Some-times	Never	Evidence used to make your judgement	Next steps
Do all staff model expected behaviour? e.g. not shouting, concentrating on tasks and showing consideration to others						
Does the curriculum allow for regular opportunities to talk with children about what good behaviour looks like?						
Do you have a visual timetable that shows children the pattern of their day/ week? Do you run through this with them daily?						
Do you prepare children for a change in routine?						
Are children receiving a consistent approach from all staff members?						
Do all staff members understand what is expected of children and what is expected of them in order to manage behaviour?						
Do staff members praise children for specific behaviours? (for example, 'excellent sitting) Is this done so that other children can hear it?						
Do staff members notice if a child is getting bored? If so do they intervene?						
Are staff members aware of which children find it difficult to get on with each other? Do they manage this?						
Are children expected to sit passively for too long?						
Are children given the chance for child-led extended play that is not interrupted by adults?						
How do you manage the use of particularly popular resources? Is there enough of these?						
Can children let you know what they do and do not like? How do you find out?						

Developing as effective behaviour management practitioners

However challenging behaviour might be of children in your care, you cannot give up and accept what you know to be unacceptable. When faced with particularly difficult circumstances, we need to do the following:

- Talk to other more experienced practitioners and ask their advice about strategies to use.
- Talk to the parents and find out what strategies they use that work for their child.
- Spend time observing the child and talking to them. Can you work out their currency, i.e. what particular strategy or reward can you use to modify their behaviour? What is it in particular that they will respond to? This might be the promise of having time with a particular activity or toy.
- Every setting will have at least one adult who is highly effective in modifying the poor behaviour of children they work with. Ask to spend some time observing and talking to them about what they do that works so successfully. You can copy and model this with your own group. The best thing about working with little children is that they will not be able to tell the difference between a highly experienced and confident practitioner and somebody who is pretending to be one!
- Follow rules and behave well yourself. For example, if all the children are gathered together in a room and the lead practitioner asks for everybody to be quiet, it is undermining for adults in the room to continue to speak. We need to lead by example and model the behaviour we expect from the children.
- Do your best to build strong bonds with the child. Instead of focusing constantly on their poor behaviour, how about focusing on improving your relationship with the child? How often do you catch them doing the right thing and praise them both privately and publicly?
- Very young children often have meltdowns when they have to stop doing something they really love. Such children need to have a warning that shortly they will be expected to leave an activity. So approach the child, get their attention and let them know that in ten minutes they will have to stop doing what they are doing. Check that they understand this and leave them. Five minutes later go back and remind them that they now have just five minutes left and that when you come back next time they will have to leave the activity. To begin with, they may struggle with this but very quickly they will find the 10 minutes warning helpful in preparing themselves to leave an activity they enjoy. Even if they make a huge fuss after the 10 minutes, you must follow through and move the child on. If you do not he or she will get the message that the more fuss they make the greater the chances of getting their own way.

- Employ a time out session for children who have not followed rules after repeated warnings or whose behaviour has been unacceptable. Time out should be somewhere quiet, away from the other children and fun activities. Children should never be put anywhere that makes them feel frightened or uncomfortable. Wherever they are, they must still be able to be seen and supervised by an adult. Before you employ this strategy, you must check with your setting as to whether this is part of their behaviour management practice.
- There may be some children whose behaviour is so extreme as to cause potential harm and risk to both children and adults alike. Under such circumstances, you must report your concerns as quickly as possible to senior managers, supported by documentary evidence, for example notes of observations or incident reports. Extreme behaviour can sometimes be an outward manifestation of particular needs. Unfortunately mainstream settings cannot always meet such needs and other support and provision may need to be considered. As an early years setting, you may well be the first people that have raised such concerns with a family about their child and therefore this must be done with great sensitivity and care. Typically, this would be a job for a senior leader.

References:

Department for children, schools and families (2010): *Inclusion Development Programme. Supporting children with Behavioural, Emotional and Social Difficulties: Guidance for practitioners in the Early Years Foundation Stage.* The National Strategies Early Years.

Early Years Foundation Stage Forum. (2015): *Behaviour management strategies.* Eyfs.info/articles.

Education Support Partnership (2015) *Behaviour management top tips.* Educationsupportpartnership.org.uk

Gordon-Smith, P. (2014): *Practice Guide: Challenging Behaviour.* Nurseryworld.co.uk.

Herefordshire Council. (2014): *Pre-school behaviour co-ordinators.* Herefordshire.gov.uk.

Suffolk County Council (2013): *Early Years and Childcare: Behaviour Support Guidance.* Suffolk.gov.uk.

The National Strategies Early Years. (2010): *Supporting children with Behavioural, Emotional and Social Difficulties: Guidance for practitioners in the Early Years Foundation Stage.* Department for Education.

Maximising boys' learning

It may seem odd that we would need to give a particular focus to boys but, year after year, early years data demonstrates that boys under perform in comparison to girls. In particular, they under perform within the areas of communication, language and literacy, and a lower percentage of boys achieve or exceed a Good Level of Development. Boys are not less able than girls but, if we are not careful, this pattern can continue into Key Stage 1, 2 and 3. It is essential that those who run early years settings plan a curriculum that meet the needs of the boys, ensuring that they achieve well.

Practitioners need to take more responsibility for creating the right conditions for boys' learning. If the outcomes we hope to see focus disproportionately on oral skills, writing and recording, the very things that boys typically find most difficult, we will be setting boys up to fail from their earliest stage of education and this needs to be avoided.

What are the right conditions to maximise their learning?

Firstly, staff will be required to get to know each boy individually. This will help to understand where their interests lie and what is likely to engage them. You need to understand their 'currency', what makes them tick, in order to plan a curriculum that will harness their interest and enthusiasm. In addition, you need to understand what they are not confident about.

Take a moment to ask yourself two questions:

- Are your activities built on their interests and strengths?
- What sort of activities are you planning for your boys each day?

Activities need to be based on their interests and strengths in order to help develop their self-confidence in their approach to learning. If we expect boys to be passive recipients of new skills and reward them for compliance, they will soon switch off and find all manner of diversions in order to avoid things they find difficult or have no interest in. We need to harness boys natural energy and their sense of enquiry to prevent disengagement. It may be worth taking some time to think about individual boys in your setting. To assist you, create a simple table to record their strengths, interests, learning style preferences and difficulties. In this way, you can carefully adjust the curriculum that you are planning for them.

Name of child	Strengths	Interests	Learning style Preferences	Difficulties	Notes

It is okay to fail

If we do not develop the curriculum that values boys' interests, strengths and preferred learning styles, they will quickly become disheartened and switch off from learning. More importantly, they will lose confidence in themselves as learners. As practitioners, we must value their ideas and efforts and plan activities that will build their confidence as learners. It is only when they are confident that they can safely experience challenge, struggle and perseverance while coming to the conclusion that these are positive things in life. They will experience failure and frustration, but they must learn that this is an important part of their learning journey and that it is necessary to develop resilience as learners. It can help to involve children in the planning and preparation of activities so that their concerns can be addressed before they attempt something new.

Guarding against stereotyping

It is important that all adults involved in boys learning ensure that both boys and girls have equal access to all activities and that these have equal value in their eyes.

Ask yourself:

- Are we really aware of the choices boys are making every day?
- How are they using the environment?
- Is there an overemphasis on certain activities and resources, do they need to be encouraged to experience others? This is equally true for girls too.

Sally Featherstone, in her 2014 book The Cleverness of Boys, identifies typical traits that early years practitioners may observe and need to respond to. It may be worth considering the following:

Typical traits	Possible practitioner responses
Boys generally concentrate best on one thing at a time	Do not ask them to do too many things at once. Give short instructions, one at a time.
If boys are required to sit and concentrate, they usually do this best after a physical activity	Timetable activities that require deep concentration after boys have had the opportunity to be involved with physical activities.
Boys generally take longer to absorb new ideas and learning, especially if it is in words or writing	Allow more time to revisit and practice. Plan opportunities to revisit and hone skills in a variety of different contexts that sustains their interest.
Boys tend to move more during learning	Do not expect boys to sit down for long periods of time. If you want them to do this, make sure it's preceded by lots of physical activity.
Very young boys are less able to recognise emotional nuance	Plan activities that model and rehearse emotions. Share stories and discuss characters emotions. Take time to explain the emotional nuance in a book or in realistic situations.

Boys are more likely to ignore voices, even those of their parents	Do not lower your expectations in terms of behaviour but do lavish them with praise when they listen and respond to. If a boy ignores you, do not give in. Get their attention and insist, in a low and calm voice, that they have to listen to you and respond accordingly.
Enjoy playground activities that involve individual running	Value the things that boys are interested in and allow them to develop these interests.
Create, and are engaged by, stories that are filled with excitement, action and ignoring victims	Value the characters and personalities that influence boys. Take time to understand the ways in which boys use superhero play as way to explore power and control. Engage with their play and narratives, this will enable you to have a positive influence.
Are primarily interested in objects and things	Plan plenty of opportunities for boys to get actively involved in projects and challenges.
Tends to have a short attention span	Give children brain breaks and opportunities for movement. Do not expect too much in one long stretch.

Watch your boys and learn what interests and excites them so that you can plan your activities to harness this enthusiasm.

Be flexible about the places, positions and situations where boys choose to work and play. Reluctant boy writers, for example, will often feel much more enthusiastic if they can see a very definite purpose and are allowed to write outside.

Ask yourself:

- Do your key workers know their boys as well as they know their girls?
- If not, what can you do as a setting to address this?
- How are you ensuring that you are creating the right conditions for boys to develop self-confidence as learners?

Typically, the things that schools value, oral communication and recording ideas in the written form, are the very things that boys really struggle with. How do we give boys positive messages about their learning and develop their confidence to risk attempting things that they know they might struggle with?

As practitioners, we must harness a boys' natural curiosity and exuberance whilst not considering it as a lack of discipline. If we do not value these traits, we risk boys switching off from their learning and potentially becoming disruptive. Think about boys whose behaviour is a concern to you. Are they badly behaved and therefore unable to learn or are they struggling with their learning and behave badly as a distraction?

One area of the curriculum that causes much frustration, for both the child and staff, is the area of developing **early writing skills**. For some boys, there is the perfect storm of finding the motor skill of writing a chore whilst also having little interest in the writing task set for them. Practitioners need to give careful consideration to planning for writing so that such boys can succeed with the physical task and are motivated to do so as the task feels real and important.

In the first instance, it is worth getting a whole class perspective on the attainment and progress in writing of the boys in your care. You may wish to complete an audit similar to the one below. Of course, gathering the same evidence about girls will be equally valuable for you.

Boys writing:

Issues for consideration	**Comments/evidence**
Boys' progress: • How is a boys' ongoing development in writing monitored during the early years foundation stage? • Are some boys making less progress in writing than in other communication, language and literacy areas, or in other areas of learning and development? • Does the attainment of any boys match that of girls? • What percentages of boys are attaining a good level of development? • What percentage of the boys will exceed? • Does this represent good progress? • How does this compare with the percentage of girls?	
Boys' writing behaviours: • Do boys and girls participate equally in writing activities? • What proportions of boys regularly choose to write? • Are there some boys who only write during adult-initiated activities? If so, who are they? • Do boys make more use of writing opportunities in some areas of your provision rather than others? • What writing activities engage boys more successfully? • Do boys see themselves as writers, engaging in writing with confidence and enthusiasm?	
The writing environment: • Are meaningful opportunities for writing built into every provision area, both in and outdoors, and particularly those where boys tend to spend more time? • Is there a wide range of attractive and interesting writing materials accessible at all times for the children? • Do children have access to a computer and are there suitable writing software programs available? • If there is an interactive whiteboard, do the children have access and are they taught how to use it?	

The role of the practitioner:	
• Do practitioners regularly monitor individual boys, to develop a picture of whether, when, where and what they write? • What individual provision is made for boys who never or rarely engage freely in writing activities? • Do practitioners regularly talk to boys about writing, to develop an understanding of their disposition and attitude to writing? For example, how confident they feel as writers, what they like or dislike about writing and their understanding of the purposes of writing? • Do practitioners regularly plan experiences and activities that will engage children in meaningful talks in order to develop their language and communication skills? • Do practitioners regularly model writing for children, both informally and in shared writing sessions? • Does teaching phonics provide children with the skill of segmenting, knowledge of the alphabetic code, and opportunities to apply their skills and knowledge to writing? • Do practitioners teach letter formation systematically? • Do practitioners offer boys opportunities to write in a wide range of forms? For example as lists, letters, signs, labels, stories, information books, messages, reports and instructions. • Do practitioners support boys' writing in freely chosen activities as well as adult-led ones? • Do practitioners support and value all boys' attempts at writing and help them to see themselves as writers? • Do practitioners respond to writing primarily in terms of content and successful communication, rather than focusing on aspects such as length, neatness or punctuation?	
Key priorities for development:	

What can settings do to maximise boys' enthusiasm and interest in writing?

Typically, boys love to be outside as much as possible. As we have already stated that we need to harness their enthusiasms and interests, it is valuable to consider how the outdoor environment can be used to encourage boys to write.

Outdoor activities that can encourage writing include:

- Whiteboards and chalkboards with an assortment of pens and chalks for them to choose from
- Chalks for writing on the playground floor

- Mark-making with sticks and mud
- An assortment of different sized paintbrushes and sponges for use with both paints and water
- Large rolls of paper, including wallpaper
- Clipboards with paper and writing tools
- Maps

If boys like to write for a purpose, ensure that in your imaginative play area and in your writing activities that boys feel that they are writing for very specific purposes. To encourage this, you could use the following:

- diaries and calendars
- telephone and address books
- postcards, invitations and tickets
- opportunities to record measurements
- signing in and out book and a visitors' book
- order forms
- maps and writing directions
- assorted paper and card (lined and unlined, different textures, specialist paper such as graph and music)
- post-it notes, stickers and stamps

The very best settings have staff that are restless and constantly reflecting on what they could do better to improve provision and outcomes for their children. In order to get an accurate perspective on the quality and success of your provision, it is important that staff pause and take stock. It may be valuable to complete an audit that considers key questions about your provision:

How effective is our provision for boys?		
Key question	**Current position**	**What we need to do next? How will we do it?**
Do we know what interests and excites each of our boys? Have key workers taken the time to get to know the children as individuals?		
Do all staff members demonstrate a consistent approach to encouraging boys to write, particularly reluctant ones?		
Does the setting have a range of resources that will interest and engage all our boys?		
Do we plan to develop an environment based on boys' strengths and helped them develop key skills?		

Do we plan activities that develop boys' concentration and encourage them to focus on something for an extended period?		
Do all practitioners involve themselves in the play experiences of boys as much as girls?		
Do we plan for a variety of active learning experiences that enable boys to problem solve, make decisions and think critically?		
Do we use a range of writing tools and materials to encourage boys in mark-making?		
Do we plan for boys to move around and experience things physically?		
If some boys work better following physical activity, do our timetables reflect this accordingly?		
What are the boys good at? What do they like?		
What do our boys do given the choice? What gets them involved?		

In conclusion:

- Invest time getting to know your boys, what interests them and plan a curriculum accordingly.
- There will always be some boys in your setting who are extremely articulate, have a passion for books and reading, love to write and are incredibly interested in the curriculum being offered to them. Use these children as role models for the others.
- Many boys love an element of competition and respond extremely well to this. Involving boys in games or activities that are goal-related can often be highly effective in engaging them.
- Are you able to engineer opportunities for boys to work alongside male adults who can act as positive role models for them?
- Make sure you have the right resources for your boys. For example, when thinking about the type of books you might have in your setting remember that boys like books that make them laugh and that appeal to their sense of mischief. They like books in a series because they provide an attractive sense of comfort and familiarity. Typically, they also like books that focus on action more than on emotions.
- If you understand what makes boys tick, what they may find hard and how to mitigate against this then you will develop a curriculum that ensures your boys will enjoy and succeed.

References:

Biddulph, S. (2015): *Raising Boys: Why Boys are Different – and How to Help Them Become Happy and Well-Balanced Men.* Harper Thorsons.

Department for children, schools and families (2007): *Confident, capable and creative.*

Supporting boys' achievements: Guidance for practitioners in the Early Years Foundation Stage. Primary National Strategy.

Department for children, schools and families (2008): *Mark making matters: Young children making meaning in all areas of learning and development. The National Strategies* Early Years.

Featherstone, S. (2014): *The Cleverness of Boys: Raising Boys' Achievement.* Featherstone Education.

Gurian, M. Stevens, K. (2010): *10 Essential Strategies for Teaching Boys Effectively.* ASCD Express.

Islington Council (2007): *Engaging Boys in the Early Years: the experiences of three Islington settings.* Islington.gov.uk.

Leslie. J. (2012): *The Gender Agenda – Boys and Literacy in the Early Years: How is boys' engagement in mark making and emergent writing influenced by the learning context and by male adult role models?*

Lincolnshire County Council (2016): *Raising boys' achievement: birth to 5.* Lincolnshire.gov.uk.

Ontario Education Excellence for All (2004): *A Practical Guide to Improving Boys' Literacy Skills.* Edu.gov.on.ca.

Children who learn English as an additional language

Children who are acquiring English as an additional language have needs that are very similar to pupils whose first language is English. However, they also have distinct needs as they are learning *through* a different language. To the untrained ear, it may appear that young children just pick up a new language as they go along; it may seem to come to them naturally, however this is not the case. Practitioners need to develop the learning environment and learning opportunities in a planned and systematic way, in order to maximise children's opportunities to acquire and develop their language skills.

Information gathering

When a child arrives in your setting who does not speak English as a first language, take time to find out as much as possible about the pupil who is learning English as an additional language (EAL). It will pay dividends in the long run. The sorts of information that may be useful to you could include:

Key question:	Notes:
What is the pupils' correct name and how is it spelt/pronounced?	
Where is the family from?	
What is the family's religion?	
What language(s) are spoken in the home?	
Who is the primary carer?	
Are there any special circumstances? E.g. is the pupil an asylum seeker/adopted/from a war zone.	
Does the pupil have older/younger siblings? Are they living at home/elsewhere?	
What is the parent/carers knowledge of English?	
What is the child's knowledge of English?	
What previous experience does the child have of early years education in the UK or elsewhere?	
Who should we contact, particularly with any urgent messages, if parent/carers do not have a good understanding of English?	

It is through interaction with adults and their peers that children learn to develop their understanding of a new language. Learning a language is a social skill. The uncertainty that comes with not being able to speak the same language as one's peers often means that young children prefer to spend time on their own, in their own little world where they are quite comfortable having conversations just with themselves and in their own language. This is not something to be overly concerned about, instead it should be seen as a necessary stage in language development. Tabors (1997) said that this silent stage is a crucial part to language acquisition. He has categorised language acquisition into the following stages. As teachers, it may be useful to identify which stage your early language learners best fit. In this way you might better be able to serve their individual needs.

Stage of language acquisition (Tabors, 1997):	Name of child:	Activities/experiences that needs to be planned for individual language development:
1. Child uses home language in second language situation		
2. When they discover that their home language does not work in this situation, children enter a non-verbal period as they collect information about the new language and perhaps spend some time with sound experimentation.		
3. Children begin to go public, using individual words and phrases in the new language.		
4. Children begin to develop productive use of the second language.		

Whilst for statistical purposes, schools often identify their EAL pupils as one group, it is important that teachers understand that not all of their EAL pupils will be at the same stage of understanding and development. They have individual needs that need to be understood and met.

Settling a new child in to your setting

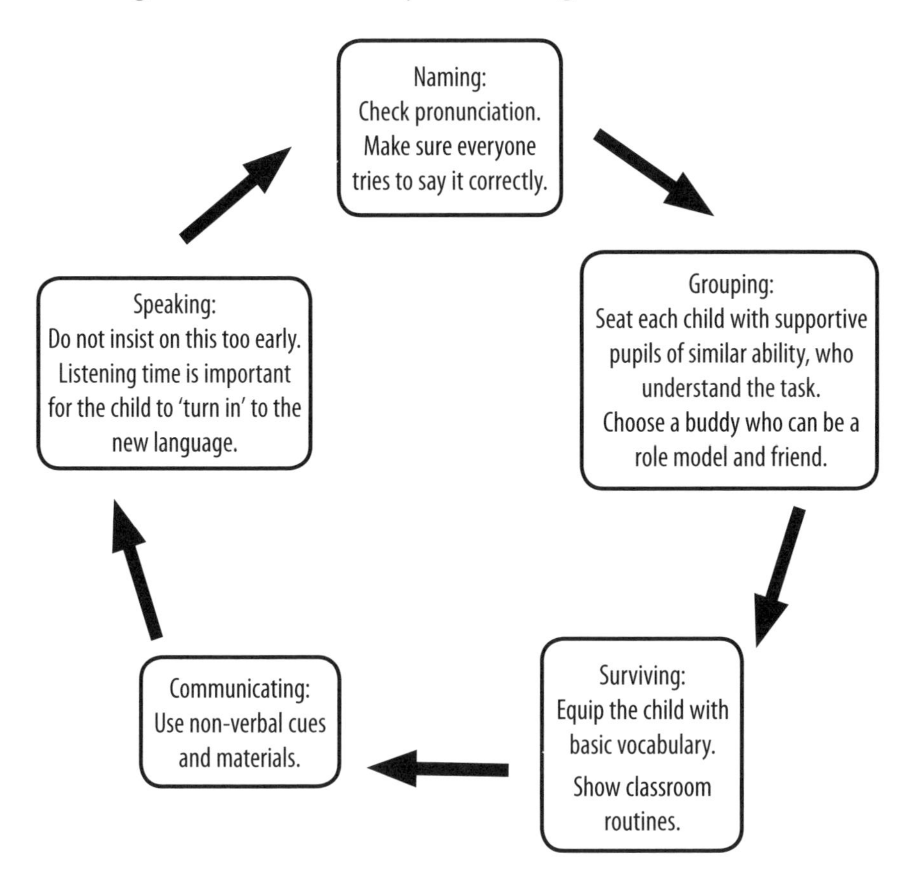

During the first few days in your setting, a child will probably watch you and the other children in order to understand what is going on. It is therefore very important to make your communication as visual as possible.

Consider using:

- Facial expressions, which you could possibly exaggerate to make it easier to understand.
- Actions, for example you could sit on the carpet to help explain what to do at story time.
- Gestures, such as thumbs up or thumbs down to indicate whether something is good or bad.

- Real objects, which you can show them so that they can associate it with the word you are saying.
- Toy objects, for example dolls furniture or toy animals.
- Pictures and photograph, these do not have to be beautifully produced.
- Their peers, children learn best from other children in the setting. Try to pair up the child with another child who will be a good language model.

As adults who direct learning opportunities and experiences, we need to ensure that children are spending the majority of their time interacting with both adults and their peers rather than engaging in solitary activities. We need to plan for them to experience rich learning activities alongside their peers so that they can pick up key vocabulary within context. This will help them to understand it's meaning, hear and see language being modelled, feel motivated to communicate themselves and begin to use language confidently and appropriately.

At the very early stages of language acquisition, children will benefit from being given visual cues to develop their understanding of particular words and phrases and help them to gain an understanding of tasks they may be expected to complete. The emphasis needs to be on speaking, listening and vocabulary. At this stage, teachers should not be too concerned about a child's ability to write.

Given that, in a earlier chapter, we have already established the need for clear and consistent routines in an early years setting, it would seem sensible to initially focus on helping children understand and use key vocabulary and phrases concerned with daily, regular routines that they will experience, words and phrases that they will need to understand and use each day. Initially this might include:

- A morning greeting and an afternoon goodbye
- Answering the register
- Asking to go to the toilet
- Lining up to leave the room
- Sitting on the carpet

Essential language and phrases that will enable the newcomer to function and express immediate needs in the first few days and weeks can include:

- Hello/goodbye
- Yes/no
- Please/thank you
- I like.../I do not like...
- I do not understand

It may also help children to have visual timetables so that they can understand the pattern of the school day and what they can expect at each time of the day throughout the week. This will help calm any anxieties.

Alongside this, they need to be immersed in a language rich environment. Adults need to offer a constant narrative and continue to talk to children even when no verbal responses are forthcoming. Early stage non-verbal responses should be acknowledged and praised; this can be quickly developed into expecting verbal responses. The 'I say/you say' approach (where an adult models a word or phrase which the child is expected to immediately repeat back) is a technique that ensures participation by the child and guarantees success and praise. Such activities are great confidence boosters because children cannot really fail. Having introduced a new word or phrase, it is then absolutely crucial that children have the opportunity to rehearse and embed this new knowledge. Children can also be encouraged to learn longer phrases and memorise sequences by the regular singing of simple songs and rhymes. Singing familiar simple songs that contain repetitive language patterns also guarantees that children can interact alongside the rest of the class.

Planning for progression

A child's understanding and use of language are assessed regularly using a systematic and detailed assessment tool.

Specific short-term goals are set for language acquisition which are understood and used by all adults. Through talk and activity, the child has language modelled, visualised and is expected to rehearse until understood and acquired.

Strengths and gaps in knowledge are identified in terms of vocabulary, understanding and the use of language.

Regularly punctuate your year with opportunities to stop and assess what children do and do not know. This will then highlight the learners' successes and identify the next steps for learning. These next steps can then be addressed through systematic planning of specific activities and learning opportunities.

Learning opportunities:	**Such as:**	**Skills taught:**
Through daily routines:	Register Lining up Play time Home time Lunch time Going to the loo	Children begin to associate particular words and phrases with what they are doing. Words and phrases are repeated daily so children become familiar with them. They see the responses that other children make and copy.
Story telling & music:	Traditional tales with a pattern, for example "The Gingerbread Man". Stories which have a repeated phrase that the class can say. It is valuable to tell stories too not just read from a book. In this way, your story telling can be adapted to individual needs. Books need to have clear illustrations. Simple songs, rhymes and phrases with rhythm	Through repetition and the identification of pattern, children begin to understand story conventions. They increase their confidence in speaking English because they know the expected response. Develops and reinforces understanding of patterns in language. Engaging in the singing of simple songs is often a child's first attempt to articulate an additional language.
First hand experience:	Cooking Using the sand pit or water tray Painting Construction Dressing or undressing	Children work alongside peers, they observe what other children are saying and may copy. They also begin to socialise and build valuable friendships. They associate specific words and phrases to what they are doing physically.
Games:	Snap I Spy Matching pairs What's the time Mr Wolf? Simon says	By repeating games which have the same rules and the same language structures, children begin to be able to use familiar repetitive vocabulary and phrases to engage with the game and describe what they are doing.

Playing games as a learning tool

Play is an essential part of any young child's learning, none more so than those learning to acquire English as an additional language. All children love to play games, and ensuring access to a wide range of games will significantly accelerate children's learning. It would be useful to audit your resources and ensure that you have range of games such as:

Game:	Language/vocabulary focus:
Match-a-balloon	Colours, dice, your turn/my turn, throw, put
Picture Lotto/matching pairs Picture snap Sound lotto Picture dominoes	Nouns and verbs
Animal and people jigsaw puzzles Size lotto Opposites	Parts of the body, clothes, animals, common nouns, language of size, back/front, push/pull, under/over
Sticker books, press and peel	Common scenes such as a school, home, farm, shop, seaside
Magnetic storyboard with story packs Guess who? What's in the bag?	Book language, common nouns, verbs physical descriptions, clothes Any set of objects, for example play food and classroom equipment
Any board or dice game	Directions, counting, taking turns

All staff who are involved with teaching EAL learners need to be aware of particular challenges that they may face. By being aware of these, staff can create opportunities to rehearse language, modelling it correctly and amending mistakes. Practitioners need to gain an understanding of the home language and how it is constructed and used. This will help to modify the learning programme correctly to ensure children's needs are being met. For example, it may be that the home language uses no personal pronouns so the child will need additional support in understanding how these are used in English. It is also helpful if practitioners understand the common, typical mistakes made by many children who are learning English. These may include the following:

Verbs	Phrasal verb	
	Modal verbs	Must, could, should, can, might, etc.
	Must, could, should, can, might, etc.	
	Subject – verb agreement	She was, not, she were
The passive voice	Object, then verb then subject	The cat was chased by the dog
Prepositions	Give information about time, manner, place and purpose	Above, below, under, next to, etc.
Adverbials	Manner of time and position	How, when, where
Noun phrases		The tall oak tree
Determiners	Determines	The, an, a, this, that, most, many, etc.
Pronouns	Stands instead of a noun/name	He, she, they, them, their, etc.
Comparison		

The golden rules for working with children who are acquiring English as an additional language

1. Children must feel that they have a secure and trusting relationship with a key adult before they are confident enough to communicate in a new language. Do all the EAL pupils in your setting have such a key person?

2. They need to feel that they are in a secure and nurturing environment.

3. Make sure all adults correctly pronounce a child's name.

4. Children learn best in meaningful contexts. Ensure that you plan to provide these.

5. Adults should offer a constant narrative when working alongside children. In this way they begin to pick up vocabulary and simple, commonly used phrases.

6. Model to correct mistakes rather than tell a child they are wrong.

7. Think carefully about how clearly you speak and at what speed. Accurate pronunciation and clear annunciation are vital. Do correct a child if they mispronounce a word and encourage them to repeat it correctly.

8. A common mistake is to speak in an exaggerated, loud fashion. This is to be avoided.

9. Repetition is crucial, not only through songs and rhymes with pattern but also through repeating and confirming when children speak to you.

10. Try to use as many open-ended questions as possible so children have the opportunity for extended responses. Those requiring a yes or no answer present a higher risk of failure.

11. Allow children time to respond to a question or direction. They need time to process what you have said and to construct a response before they say it.

12. Learning an additional language is exhausting. Respect this when working with very little children and do not expect too much from them.

13. First hand experiences provide the most effective context for learning language. Ensure your setting provides a range of these for children. They do not have to cost anything. Cooking, gardening, tidying are all activities rich in relevant vocabulary that children can recreate and rehearse in role-play.

As of September 2016, schools must inform the government of each child's country of birth, nationality and their level of proficiency in English if it is not their first language. The five new codes to assess EAL pupils are as follows:

A NEW TO ENGLISH	The pupil may: Use first language for learning and other purposes Remain completely silent in the classroom Be copying/repeating some words or phrases Understand some everyday expressions in English but may have minimal or no literacy in English Needs a considerable amount of EAL support
B EARLY ACQUISITION	The pupil may: Follow day-to-day social communication in English and participate in learning activities with support Begin to use spoken English for social purposes Understand simple instructions and can follow narrative/accounts with visual support Have developed some skills in reading and writing Have become familiar with some subject specific vocabulary Still needs a significant amount of EAL support to access curriculum
C DEVELOPING COMPETENCE	The pupil may: Participate in learning activities with increasing independence Be able to express self orally in English, but structural inaccuracies are still apparent Be able to follow abstract concepts and more complex written English Literacy will require ongoing support, particularly for understanding text and writing. Requires ongoing EAL support to access curriculum fully.
D COMPETENT	Oral English developing well, enabling successful engagement in activities across the curriculum Can read and understand a wide variety of texts Written English may lack complexity and contain occasional evidence of errors in structure Needs some support to access subtle nuances of meaning, to refine English usage, and to develop abstract vocabulary Needs some/occasional EAL support to access complex curriculum material and tasks
E FLUENT	Can operate across the curriculum to a level of competence equivalent to a pupil who uses English as first language. Operates without EAL support across the curriculum Bilingual

References:

Department for education and skills (2007): *Excellence and Enjoyment: Learning and teaching for bilingual children in the primary years.* Primary National Strategy.

Dorset Early Years Team (2012): *Children learning English as an additional language (EAL).* Dorsetforyou.gov.uk.

Drury, R. Robertson, L. (2008): Strategies for early years practitioners. National Association for Language Development in the Curriculum.

Edwards, V. (1995): *Speaking and Listening in Multicultural Classrooms.* Multilingual Matters.

Gloucestershire County Council (2006): *Gloucestershire Race Equality and Diversity Service: English as an Additional Language – A Guide to Working with Children in Early Years Settings.* Irespect.net.

Hall, D. (1995): *Assessing the Needs of Bilingual Pupils: Living in Two Languages.* David Fulton Publishers Ltd.

Herefordshire Council (2014): *EAL: A Guide to Working with Children in the Early Years.* Herefordshire.gov.uk.

Tabors, P. (2002): *Language and literacy for all children.* Department of Health and Human Services, Administration for Children and Families.

Assessment and Observation

Apart from the daily on-going formative assessment that all practitioners make about children in their care, there are certain important summative assessments that have to be completed at particular points in a young child's life.

Progress check at age 2

'When a child is aged between two and three, practitioners must review their progress and provide parents and/or carers with a short, written summary of their child's development in the prime areas. This progress check must identify the child's strengths and any areas where the child's progress is less than expected. If there are significant emerging concerns, or an identified special educational need or disability, practitioners should develop a targeted plan to support the child's future learning and development involving parents and/or carers and other professionals (for example, the provider's Special Educational Needs Co-ordinator or health professionals) as appropriate'. Each child's level of development must be assessed against the early learning. Practitioners must indicate whether children are meeting expected levels of development, or if they are exceeding expected levels, or not yet reaching expected levels ('emerging'). This is the EYFS Profile.

Ref: EYFS Statutory Framework 2014

Assessment at the end of the EYFS – the Early Years Foundation Stage Profile (EYFSP):

In the final term of the year in which the child reaches age five, and no later than 30 June in that term, the EYFS profile must be completed for each child. The profile provides parents and carers, practitioners and teachers with a well-rounded picture of a child's knowledge, understanding and abilities, their progress against expected levels and their readiness for Year 1. The profile must reflect: ongoing observation; all relevant records held by the setting; discussions with parents and carers, and any other adults whom the teacher, parent or carer judges can offer a useful contribution.

Ref: EYFS Statutory Framework 2014

It is important that staff members that are making judgements about children have criteria against which they can make these informed decisions. All practitioners will of course use the 'Development Matters in the EYFS' (DfE 2012) as the document to refer to when making judgements and building a picture of what children can and cannot do.

Practitioners should be in a constant cycle of observation, assessing and recording children's achievements. It is important to understand where each child is positioned against given criteria because:

- **We are better able to demonstrate progress.** We regularly assess what children can do or record moments when they acquire a new skill, vocabulary or understanding. We are able to monitor their progress over time and check that it is as it should be, that children are meeting appropriate milestones at the relevant age.
- **We gain a detailed understanding of what children can and cannot do.**
- **We can identify what they need to do to improve** and, therefore, plan opportunities for them to rehearse and acquire appropriate skills, knowledge and understanding.
- **We can be alert to any areas of significant concern** (e.g. a Special Educational Need or Disability-SEND) regarding meeting their developmental milestones and make a plan to address specific needs.

Effective practice does not take a scattergun, 'one size fits all' approach to teaching in early years.

In the least effective settings, activities are planned regardless of what each child may need or where children's interests may lie. In such situations, practitioners ask themselves **'what do I want children to do?'** Learning under these circumstances is limited because it is all about the *activity* and not the learning.

In the best settings, practitioners start with asking themselves **'what do I want the children to learn?'** They then consider what type of activity might be best employed to achieve effective learning for the child.

All early years practitioners should use the following cycle to plan the curriculum for their children:

1. Practitioners **observe** their children both formally and informally.

2. They **assess** what children can do, what they struggle with and their attitudes to learning.

3. They **record** important information about the child that helps build a picture of their abilities and understanding of a comprehensive range of areas.

4. **Reporting**: They share this information with colleagues and families. There is information exchange that helps to further build the accuracy of the picture.

5. Practitioners use the information they have gathered to **plan** a bespoke programme for the child to help them rehearse, practise and acquire skills and knowledge.

6. Planning is used to create learning opportunities that will be **delivered** to children that specifically meet their needs and interests.

Practitioner records the child's responses to the activity or situation and the cycle starts again.

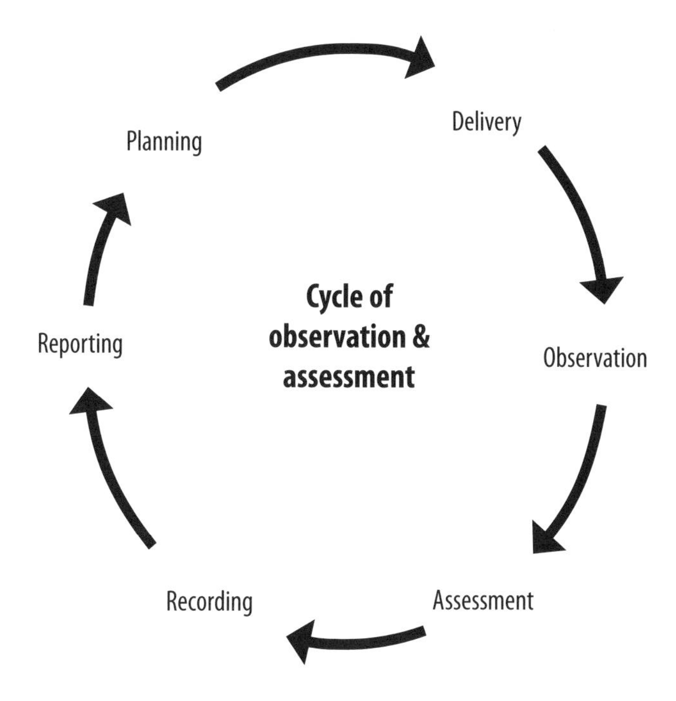

Assessing and recording in this way means that practitioners can more easily identify children's strengths (where they exceed chronological expectation) and where they might be experiencing difficulties (where they are failing to meet the expectation).

Characteristics of effective learning, observing how a child is learning:

Playing and exploring (engagement):	Active learning (motivation):	Creating and thinking critically (thinking):
Finding out and exploring: Showing curiosity about objects, events and people Using senses to explore the world around them Engaging in open-ended activity Showing particular interests	Being involved and concentrating: Maintaining focus on the activity for a period of time Showing high levels of energy, fascination Not easily distracted Paying attention to detail	Having their own ideas: Thinking of ideas Finding ways to solve problems Finding new ways to do things
Playing with what they know: Pretending objects are things from their experience Representing their experiences in play Taking on a roll in their play Acting out experiences with other people	Keeps on trying: Persisting with activity when challenges occur Showing a belief that more effort or a different approach will pay off Bouncing back after difficulties	Making links: Making links and noticing patterns in their experience Making predictions Testing their ideas Developing ideas of grouping, sequences, cause and effect
Being willing to 'have a go': Initiating activities Seeking a challenge Showing a 'can do' attitude Taking a risk, engaging in new experiences and learning by trial and error	Enjoying achieving what they set out to do: Showing satisfaction in meeting their own goals Being proud of how they accomplished something, not just the end result Enjoy meeting challenges for their own sake rather than external rewards or praise	Choosing ways to do things: Planning, making decisions and how to approach a task, solve a problem and reach a goal Checking how well their activities are going Changing strategy as needed Reviewing how well the approach worked

Ref: Development Matters in the EYFS, DFE, 2012.

References:

Department for Education (2013): Early years outcomes: a non-statutory guide for practitioners and inspectors to help inform understanding of child development through the early years. Foundationyears.org.uk.

West Sussex Education (2006): *Effective Practice: Observation, Assessment and Planning.*

Early Years Matters (2016): *Observation, Assessment & Planning.*

School Readiness

UNICEF's description of "school readiness" consists of three pillars: a child's readiness for school, a school's readiness for children and a family's readiness for school. Together, these three pillars maximise each child's likelihood of success as they progress through their time in school.

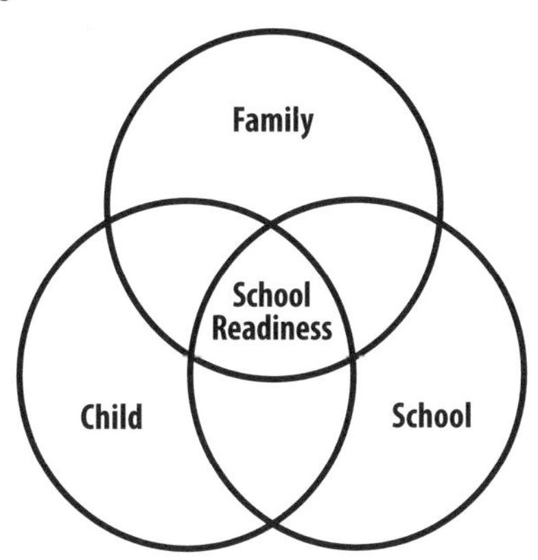

Ofsted's Chief Inspector, Sir Michael Wilshaw, used an example in his 2014 annual report on early years, which was originally given by Frank Field in his 2010 report "The Foundation Years", to highlight the importance of school readiness. He cited a checklist of 10 skills that every child should possess by the time they start school, this includes:

- To sit still and listen
- To be aware of other children
- To understand the word 'no' and the boundaries it sets for behaviour
- To understand the word 'stop' and that such a phrase might be used to prevent danger
- To be toilet-trained and be able to go to the loo
- To recognise their own name
- To speak to an adult to ask for help
- To be able to take off their coat and put on shoes
- To talk in sentences
- To open and enjoy a book

Whilst these provide a helpful guide for parents, school readiness requires a rather more sophisticated approach from staff involved in supporting children and their families at this important milestone. School readiness not only requires preparation for the child but parents and schools also need to consider *their* readiness. They need to consider how *they* have prepared for this moment to ensure transition into school is smooth and successful. There needs to be highly effective cooperation between the school staff, families and the child.

In Ofsted's survey "Are you ready? Good practice in school readiness" from April 2014, best practice was highlighted in terms of how to prepare the most disadvantaged and vulnerable children for starting school. Whilst the focus was on highly effective practice in deprived areas, there was a great deal of advice that would equally apply to all children starting school, this includes:

- Where a setting develops close partnerships with families, they are more likely to develop a mutual understanding of expectations.
- Effective settings have specific programs of support and appropriate interventions to help children develop their speaking, listening and communication skills if these are seen to be lagging behind those of others. These are adult-led to discreet sessions for groups of children.
- Communication development is accelerated when every member of staff speaks clearly and understands the importance of promoting opportunities for children to speak in sentences, initiate questions and offers children opportunities for imaginative role play scenarios.
- Pupil premium funding is used to ensure the early identification and specialist support children from their starting points.
- Settings very quickly complete and accurate assessment of the child's starting point or baseline.
- Settings recognise and respond to any common areas of weakness in children starting points within their community.

School readiness: the child

Along with the 10 skills stated above, there are many other things that will be useful for children to have some knowledge or skill of before they start school.

One of the most difficult lessons for a new starter is to realise that he or she is not the centre of attention. They have to share toys, take turns and cannot always have the attention of the adult.

Children also need to be able to follow simple instructions and directions whilst being able to develop their concentration and staying power, particularly when something is challenging. So often children arrive in school with 'grazing' habits, moving from one activity to another in quick succession, never sustaining interest or showing determination. If they do not get an immediate rush then they move on. This is something that can have a detrimental effect on learning and staff members need to work hard to develop a child's stamina and resilience.

What is it that we want to develop in children to ensure they get the very best out of starting school?

We want our new learners to:

- Be curious, ask questions and be confident enough to access everything that is on offer.
- Feel excited, confident and enthusiastic about their learning.
- Know that when they come across a problem, they can find a solution, remain resilient and take risks, if necessary.
- Feel happy about coming to school; they know they are special and that their efforts are acknowledged and rewarded.
- Develop their social skills and abilities to communicate with others.
- Feel valued as an individual and a member of the group.
- Gain a broad range of knowledge, skills and vocabulary through everyday experiences.

You need to ask the following questions:

- How much of the curriculum and the interaction with staff in your setting support the development of the attributes listed above?
- Are there areas of the curriculum that you need to improve?
- Are the ways in which you interact and communicate with children good enough to develop these characteristics?
- What more do you need to do?
- Once baseline assessments have been completed, and any gaps have been identified, it is important that a program is quickly put in place to address the child's needs.

School readiness: families

Parents are key in ensuring a child starts school confidently. It is their primary responsibility to make sure that the child is well prepared although they will benefit from advice and guidance from school staff. As a parent, consider the following as ways to ensure the transition to school is effective:

- Understand that you are your child's most important role model so lead by example, if you are positive and enthusiastic about school your child will be too.
- Rehearse the school routine. If they need to be up, eating breakfast and dressed by 8.30am in order to attend school on time, it would be sensible to get into this routine a few weeks before the term starts.

- Discuss school rules and how important it is to follow them.
- Role-play school situations, for example by pretending to be a pupil and needing to put your hand up to speak.
- Read with your child every night.
- Label all their clothes, including their socks.
- Make sure your child is used to sharing.
- Make sure your child is used to doing as he or she is told at a speed and time dictated by the adult.
- Does your child have self-knowledge, especially about any medical or dietary needs they might have?
- With the introduction of free school meals for pupils in key stage 1, can your child use cutlery properly? Can they sit at a dining table for a sustained period? If you would prefer to supply a packed lunch, can your child open a yoghurt pot or peel a banana?
- Do not give your child zips, buttons or laces if they cannot do them up by themselves.
- Ensure your child says 'please' and 'thank you'.
- Encourage your child to try new things and different ways of doing things.
- Can they wipe their own nose with a tissue, and know when to do so?
- Is your child used to being separated from you? If they are not, they need to have some experience of this before term begins.
- Establish a good sleeping routine.

School readiness: staff

School readiness is not about expecting all children to have reached a particular standard before they start school. Although there is a basic minimum that we might want all children to achieve, in reality this will not be the case. Children develop at different rates and in different ways. Readiness will not happen at the same time for all children. For school staff, readiness is about knowing about each unique child so that the school is ready to welcome children and deliver an appropriate curriculum, regardless of an individual's starting point.

As a school, do you have your own checklist of ten or 15 skills that you wish your children to be able to do before they start school? These need to be communicated to parents with enough notice for them to address issues in plenty of time. Priorities will be slightly different but might include:

- Being able to get dressed independently and quickly, this will make PE lessons much less stressful for both the child and the staff

- Recognising rhyming sounds
- Knowing some nursery rhymes and traditional tales
- Speaking clearly
- Listening to a story without interrupting
- Counting to ten
- Knowing the colours and be able to sort objects based on colour, size or shape
- Being able to throw, catch and bounce a ball
- Be confident enough to seek help from an adult when necessary
- Being able to hold a pencil correctly
- Demonstrate listening skills and be able to pay attention to a subject or stimulus for a period of time
- Understand and respond to the boundary setting

Schools must also take into consideration and be sympathetic to any differences in ability, culture, language and prior experience. This is in particular for those children who may have special educational needs or disabilities.

Children with special educational needs or disabilities

Transition for children with special educational needs or disabilities (SEND) is even more crucial. The consequences of getting this wrong could be significant and so it is important that staff invest heavily in transition arrangements for such children.

- If there are any multi-agency meetings being held prior to the child starting with you, make sure somebody from your setting is able to attend. You will gain information and knowledge from key workers who know the child well which will prove to be invaluable.
- If any adaptations are required, these will need to be planned for well in advance. Be aware of any specialist equipment that is required and any staff training. Such issues need to be addressed before the child starts at your setting.
- Gather together all relevant information about the child. Check it accurately with other agencies and with the parents too. Certain information, relating to their learning or how they will operate during the day, must be shared with all adults that will be working with the child.
- Understand the strategies that have worked well in other settings and try to replicate these where it is possible. Use similar, or ideally the same, equipment and activities, at least initially. This gives the child a sense of familiarity, consistency and security.
- Prepare to be more flexible in terms of their start at your setting. It may require more time and effort than that given to other children.

Home visiting

Investing in this opportunity to visit children in their homes and meet with their families is recognised as hugely advantageous to the child, their parents and the staff who will be working with the child. Staff members are likely to see the children at their most comfortable and relaxed and it is an opportunity to start building relationships with parents and carers. Staff can reassure children and their parents regarding any anxieties or concerns they may have.

In order to prepare parents and children for the meeting, many settings will send out short, informative leaflet telling parents how they can get the best out of the visit. Information could include the following:

Dos and do not's of preparing for a home visit:

DO

- See this as a valuable opportunity to get to know the teacher, and vice versa, on a one-to-one basis. Being on home ground is designed to make you feel more comfortable.
- Use the visit to raise any concerns you or your child may have. This may be about their learning, social skills, strengths and anxieties.
- Make sure you communicate any information regarding the family context or parenting responsibilities. This is particularly important if the child is not living with both their parents.
- Inform the visitor on things your child is particularly good at and what they are particularly interested in.
- Prepare your child for the visit. You can tell them that their new teacher is coming to visit.
- Prepare a particular book, a toy or a piece of news that they would like to share with their visitor when they arrive?
- Tell your child in advance that while the visitor is at their home, the television needs to be turned off. Do not wait to have a row about this in front of the visitor.

DO NOT

- Worry about what the teacher was going to think of your house or its state of cleanliness, this is not the purpose of the visit.
- Let the appointment overrun. Teachers will be seeing a number of people on the same day and so cannot stay too long at anyone's home.
- Some of the most effective practice involves giving children photo books to share at home prior to the start of the new term. The books could contain photos of the staff they must get to know, their classrooms and photomaps

of the school, where trays and coat hooks are located. These booklets can be left with families so that children can have the opportunity to rehearse and remember important aspects of school life.

- For staff involved in home visits, it is always useful to get feedback once the child has started your setting. It may help to ask questions such as:
- Was the home visit useful?
- Was there anything that the parents did not like about it?
- What could the setting do better next time?

References:

Hampshire County Council (2013): *School Readiness.* Hants.gov.uk.

Joshi, L (2010): *Raising Children: the Primary Years: Everything Parents Need to Know – from Homework and Horrid Habits to Screentime and Sleepovers.* Pearson Life.

Ofsted. (2014): *Are you ready? Good practice in school readiness.* Gov.uk.

Potter, S. (2012): *Creating School Readiness.* Foundationyears.org.uk.

Professional Association for Childcare and Early Years. (2013): *What does "school ready" really mean?* Pacey.org.uk.

Unicef (2012): *School Readiness: a conceptual framework.* Unicef.org.

Role of key workers

In the EYFS framework glossary, the key person is defined as "the named member of staff with whom the child has more contact than other adults. This adult shows a special interest in a child through close personal interaction day-to-day."

In every setting, each child must be assigned a key person. The key person must:

- Help ensure that every child's learning and care is tailored to meet their individual needs.
- Seek to engage and support parents and/or carers in guiding their child's development at home.
- Help families to engage with more specialist support, if it is appropriate to do so.

The key worker is a familiar figure that is accessible and available as a point of contact for parents; one who builds relationships with the child and parents or carers. This does not mean though that a child only ever works with one adult and that that adult sticks to them like glue. Part of the role of the key worker is to develop children's confidence to build relationships with children and other adults in the setting, so that they become more independent. When children feel happy and secure in this way they are confident to explore and to try out new things.

When a child begins to attend a setting, the care provider must inform the parent/carer of the key person's name and explain what the role involves.

The role of the key worker

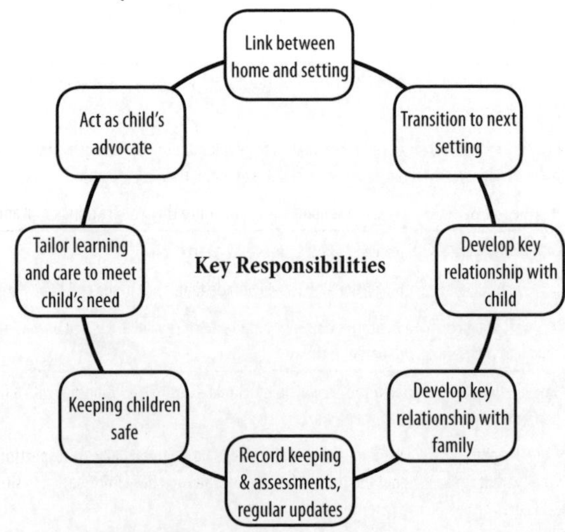

Key features of role:	What this might look like in practice:
Develop a key relationship with a child	Greet them each morning. Make sure you have at least one one-on-one fairly lengthy conversation with them each day. See them off at the end of the day. Make sure they have everything they need. Make daily, regular observations about various aspects of their learning as well as physical, emotional end social presentation.
Develop key relationship with family/carers	Complete a home visit before a child starts in the setting. Use informal meetings and events to develop the relationship with families. Be available at the start and end of each day to meet and greet parents or carers. Use this opportunity to share and receive any important information. It is important to share good news about children; let the family know how much you genuinely like and care for their child. As you begin to get to know a child, or observe changes, share these with the parents. Do they agree? Have they made similar observations?
Record keeping and assessments	Make daily regular observations about various aspects of their learning as well as their physical, emotional and social presentation. Record any milestone development, important things that they say or do compared to the EYFS criteria. Include any new information about the child in their records. Update your records regularly.
Keeping children safe	Ensure that the environment and practice at your setting is compliant and keeps children safe. Report any concerns about unsafe practice and record when and to whom these concerns have been raised. If you have any concerns about a child's care or that they may be in danger, report these to the designated safeguarding officer and record when and to whom these concerns have been raised.
Tailor learning and care to meet a child's needs	As you get to understand a child's personality, you will know what makes them tick and you can use this to get the best out of them. Not only should you engineer opportunities to develop children's strengths but you should also help them to address any areas of under confidence or inability. It is the role of the key worker to support the child, notice them doing things well and praise them.
Act as child's advocate	Do you always act with the child's best interests at heart? Do you speak up if you think a decision is being made that is not in the child's best interests? It is vital that you strike the correct balance between offering advice based on your relationship with a child and interfering with parental choice.
Link between home and setting	This relationship is crucial. If you are not able to build a positive relationship with a family then it is probably best to assign a new key worker. The relationship between home and school needs to be nurtured daily. Be respectful of and interested in what parents tell you about the child at home and when you have information to share, particularly if it is likely to be something parents do not want to hear. Make sure you do this in a sensitive way, acknowledging their feelings and being positive and confident about the way forward.

How many children should be assigned to a key person?

Although it is for the school or setting to decide how many children to assign to each key person, it would seem sensible to use the EYFS framework staffing ratios as a guide (refer to pages 21 to 24 of the EYFS framework). For example, children aged two in an EYFS setting should have at least one member of staff for every four children. It would seem sensible that a key worker in a setting catering to this age group should have no more than four children for whom they are responsible.

It is also worth considering the skills and experience of people before assigning numbers of children to staff. Less experienced staff should receive extra support with their key person responsibilities. Ratios will also depend on the individual children's needs. If there is a child who requires a great deal of additional support, due to SEND issues or behavioural challenges perhaps, they may need a dedicated key person who works solely with them. In extreme situations the child may require two key people.

Induction for key workers

Before starting at a setting, it is vital that new staff members are given some induction, this should include an introduction to the policies and practice of the setting. An effective induction ensures that new staff can quickly learn the settings policies, processes and practices so continuity is preserved for children and staff who can feel confident that they are doing a good job. Time invested in a comprehensive induction programme will pay dividends for both the new staff member and the setting.

When planning an induction programme, it is useful to consider what it is that you wish to achieve and then plan the best way for doing this. The following framework for an induction programme may be useful when considering how to shape one for your setting:

Broad themes:	**Topics you may wish to cover:**
General introduction to the setting	A tour of the building and outside areas, provision of locker space, explanation of expectations regarding when to be in work, including shifts and meetings and an introduction to other staff members, children and parents.
Personal information	An emergency contact and information on their next of kin, a P45 from their previous job, their home address and contact numbers, a check to see if their qualifications/training is completed, their proof of ID and a DBS check.
Policies and procedures	A job description, a copy of the staff handbook, their contract of employment, performance management procedures, professional development entitlement and any additional policies that they need to read and understand.
Expectations	Details of a dress code or uniform, a confidentiality agreement, information on the role of the role model and key worker and defining what you expect in terms of attitude, communication and their telephone manner.

The structure of the setting	Explanation of routines, staff structure and what services are provided.
Working with colleagues and parents	Highlighting the importance of professionalism, respect, support and supervision. The significance of communication to voice general concerns, difficulties and complaints.Information on staff members roles, the designated safeguarding officer, how to welcome parents and daily feedback.
Working with children	The importance of developing positive relationships, dealing with challenging behaviour, individual observations and plans, daily record keeping and routines.
Policies and procedures	Read through the policies given followed by a question session, ensure that they sign and date individual policies to show they have been read and understood, explain all records that are kept in relation to individual children, share observation and record keeping sheets, share planning sheets and explain how these are used.
Child protection	Book staff members on to the appropriate training and introduce them to the designated safeguarding officer. Gather any certificates that demonstrate previous training and a date of when it was completed. Familiarise all staff with key documents and reporting procedures.
Health and safety	Importance of personal and child hygiene, vaccinations (both adults and child), cleaning and maintenance, first-aid supplies, who the first-aid contact is, what the evacuation routine, fire drill, security routine is, domestic routine duties food safety and safe handling, sick leave and reporting absence.
Using equipment and resources	Safe use, care and storage of equipment, procedures for use of equipment, safe food storage and keeping an inventory.
Record keeping	Timesheets and registers, daily records for children, accident forms, service records – cleaning schedules, health and safety issues and staff responsibility for reporting issues of health and safety.

As a staff member, if may be useful to look at the table above and check whether you are familiar with the information suggested. If there happens to be anything you are not familiar with, it would be prudent to approach your line manager in order to find out any information you do not yet know.

The importance of record keeping

Assessment is a frequent and on-going process throughout the early years foundation stage. The principle strategy for assessing young children's development and learning is observation. Based on the knowledge and understanding learned from observations, practitioners respond appropriately and plan for a child's next steps. However, it is crucial that key workers strike an appropriate balance between making observations and interacting with children. The majority of your day should be spent working with and talking to children, not writing observations or taking photos as evidence.

"Assessment should not entail prolonged breaks from interaction with children, nor require excessive paperwork. Paperwork should be limited to that which is absolutely necessary to promote children's successful learning and development." – The Statutory Framework for the Early Years Foundation Stage 2014.

Key workers, other staff members, parents and any additional agencies, that have had an involvement with the child, should be involved in the creation of a record of a child's development and progress. In this way a comprehensive record is produced that will both inform current planning for the child and, in addition, be a valuable source of information when the child transitions to another room, setting or school.

- Do make sure that all staff members have had training in how to keep accurate and useful records. It may help to ask the following questions:
- Do they know the sorts of things they should comment on?
- Is there a collective pro forma that all staff must use?
- Does this pro forma guide staff about what to look for and how to record information?
- Is the system of observation and record keeping manageable?
- Is it shared with and contributed to by others?

It is all about relationships

What makes a highly effective key worker is the ability to communicate really effectively with whom they come into contact. They are able to establish excellent relationships with colleagues, the child and the child's family so that everyone is working together in the best interests of the child.

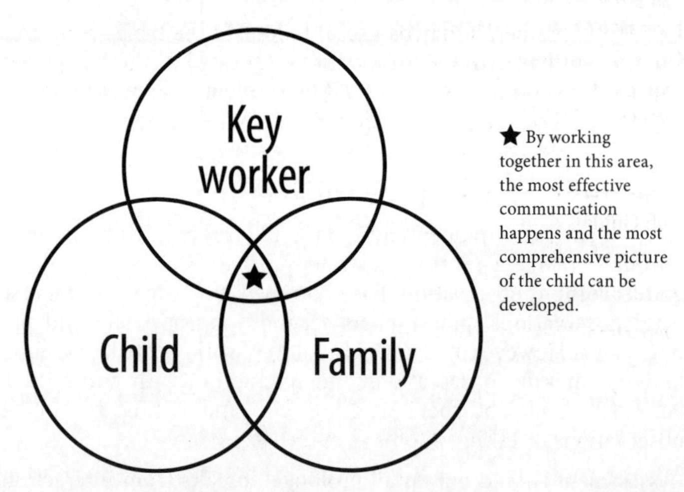

Once staff members are well established in your setting, it is prudent to regularly review how effective your practice is. Is there more you could do? Are there things that could be improved?

It may be useful to complete the following audit to identify the next steps for improvement:

How effective is the practice of our key workers?

Key question:	Current position:	Next steps for the setting:
How do parents and carers work with staff during a child's settling in period?		
How do staff members make sure that children feel secure when the time comes to say goodbye to their parent/carer and the child must stay in the nursery/reception class alone?		
How are care routines like going to the toilet, getting dressed, eating, resting or sleeping managed for children so that they feel personalised rather than institutional and uncaring?		
How are children comforted when they feel distressed or tired?		
If a child's behaviour is challenging, how do you ensure that a limited number of staff, who have a trusting relationship with the child, manage difficult incidents?		
Does each key worker know the children they are responsible for really well? Do they know their individual personality traits, their little quirks and their "currency" that you can use to get the very best out of them?		
Do we support children both by what we say and by what we do? For example, does your face light up when your key children arrive at the setting each day?		
Are all children in the setting offered emotional security through a calm and consistent approach from all staff?		
Are the key workers aware of a child's cultural heritage, their family backgrounds and situations? Do they respond accordingly? Do they keep careful records that are regularly updated?		
Do you plan time for each key person to work with parents so that they really know and understand the children in their key group?		

Ref: Guidance: the key person in reception classes and small nursery settings, The National Strategies Early Years, 2008

References:

Department for Education (2014): *Statutory Framework for the early years foundation stage: Setting the standards for learning, development and care for children from birth to five.* Gov.uk.

Early Years Matters (2016): *Key Person and Attachment.* Earlyyearsmatters.co.uk.

Early Years Foundation Stage (2011): *Principles into Practice.*

Grenier, J. Elfer, P. Morton, J. Wilson, D. and Dearnley, K. (2008): *Guidance: the key person in reception classes and small nursery settings.* The National Strategies Early Years.

Department for Education (2005): *Sure Start: Key Elements of Effective Practice.* Primary National Strategy.

Islington Children's Services (2016): *Observation, Assessment and Record Keeping in the Foundation Stage.* Islington.gov.uk.

Leadership in early years' settings

Sir Michael Wilshaw (Ofsted HMCI) believes that good leadership in early years is something that can be judged by answering one simple question: "are children ready for school or not at the end of their early years education?"

He goes on in his report to state that what makes a setting good or outstanding is strong leadership.

Any leader of any early years setting would do well to take a look at his 2013 report titled: "Achieving and maintaining high quality early years provision: getting it right first time". This should be used as a starting point to review one's own setting against what is defined as the best practice:

Using "Achieving and maintain high quality early years provision: getting it right first time" to evaluate provision and identify required improvements in leadership.		
Key question:	**Current position in setting:**	**Next steps for setting:**
Do leaders in the setting have a high enough expectation? Is there a strong sense of purpose with high aspirations for children's achievement?		
Do leaders take steps to ensure they are well qualified and experienced? Do your staff members have a combination of relevant qualifications, accredited training and relevant experience? Do leaders understand precisely what good and outstanding teaching looks like and how children learn best?		
Do leaders communicate effectively and lead by example? Do you inspire your staff? Are you explicit about what you want to see and why? Are leaders able to explain to staff why certain strategies work and others do not?		
Do leaders make the right changes at the right time? Is it possible to overcome barriers to ensure the best possible provision for children? Are leaders able to prioritise what needs to be done, focusing first on the things that would make the most difference to children's learning? Do you secure the agreement of staff when making change? Do you allow enough time for new initiatives and changes to become firmly established? Do you encourage and expect all staff to contribute ideas and suggestions for improvement?		

Do you identify strengths and weaknesses of the settings work? Does your self-evaluation involve input from staff, children and families?		
Do leaders always focus on what could be expected of children at different ages and stages of development and on their progress?		
Do leaders regularly ask: What is it like for the children here? What difference are you making, and how do we know?		

In order to know how and what to improve, leaders within settings must involve themselves regularly in self-evaluation. Self-evaluation is not something that is done only once. In the best settings, staff members are continually reflecting on their practice, the children's experience and the outcomes that children achieve. The most effective early years leaders are restless, regularly asking themselves "what more can we do and what can we do better?"

Cycle of Self-Evaluation:

Leaders must create a culture within which they regularly reflect upon and review what they are doing.

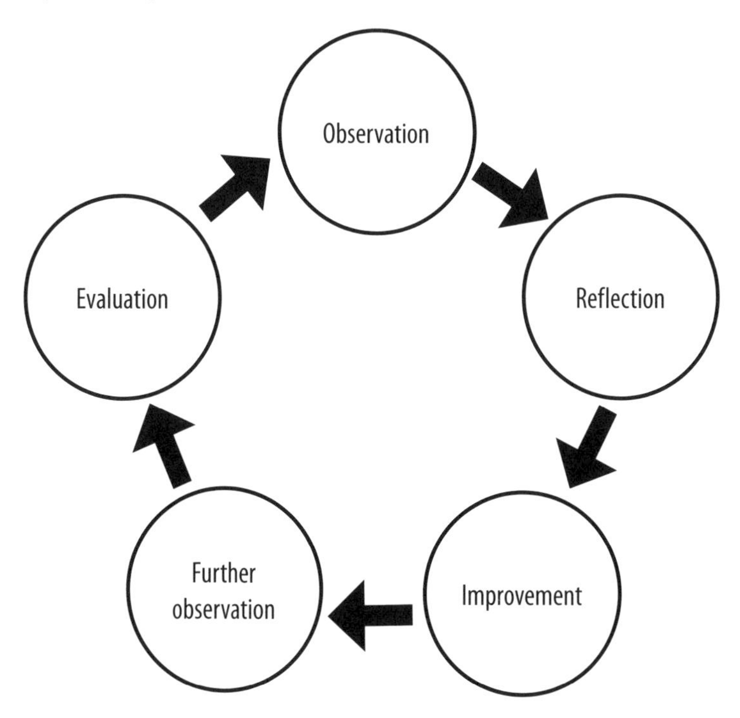

How can early years leaders create an environment of constant self-reflection and evaluation?

- They can have frequent meetings that focus specifically on how to improve the quality of learning and teaching.
- They should give staff the chance to visit other settings, which are judged good or outstanding, so that they can see what best practice looks like and combine ideas.
- They can give staff members the opportunity each week to reflect on the impact of their work and consider how well children have learned.
- They must be committed to and invested in professional development; this does not have to cost a fortune as settings can join together with others and share their own best practice.
- They should encourage and facilitate input from parents and carers.
- They can ensure all leaders are up-to-date with new national regional or local initiatives and what might these mean for the setting.
- They could make use of the expertise of an external adviser who will offer both challenge and advice to senior leaders, this does not need to cost because it could be completed as part of a reciprocal arrangement with another setting. This is particularly useful for settings with no formal governance arrangements.
- They can use governing bodies to act as a critical friend to offer both support and challenge for self-improvement.

It might also be useful for you to access the online self-evaluation form which is available from the Ofsted website:

www.gov.uk/government/publications/early-years-online-self-evaluation-form-sef-and-guidance-for-providers-delivering-the-early-years-foundation-stage

How do leaders build an effective early years team?

Staffing: Effective teams are built from experienced and well-qualified staff members that have a secure knowledge of how young children learn best.

Induction: When a setting employs a new member of staff, it is crucial that they invest significant amounts of time and energy in their induction. Staff members have to understand the particular way that the setting does things, such as its policies and protocols. They need to gain a clear understanding very quickly of what is acceptable behaviour and practice. Through observation of the best practitioners they will see:

- What is expected of them

- How they should interact with and talk to children
- What is expected of them in terms of curriculum planning
- How they are expected to contribute to the work of the team
- How they communicate as key workers with families and carers

Never underestimate the impact of thorough induction. It may frustrate the new member of staff that they can not get just get on with their job, but taking things slowly and carefully at the start will pay dividends in the long term. At the same time, take the opportunity to talk to the new member of staff about their first impressions of the setting. You can ask them:

- Is it welcoming?
- Has the induction been useful?
- What is their impression of the setting in terms of resources, interaction with children and parents, expectations of staff and effective communication?

Once a staff member is established, they no longer see the setting with fresh eyes so take the opportunity to find out about their initial impressions of the setting and learn from them.

Performance management: Staffing is the biggest financial investment of your setting and therefore it is crucial that staff performance is managed effectively.

The best leaders hold staff to account. Where staff performance is poor or where appropriate outcomes for children are not secured, they accept no excuses and insist individuals take responsibility for the quality of their practice and the impact this can have on a child's achievement. Highly effective settings establish a regular cycle, which includes observations, work scrutiny, feedback and training. This ensures that staff members are well supported in becoming highly effective practitioners.

The year also needs to be punctuated with opportunities to sit with each staff member and reflect on what they are doing well and what might need to be improved. What are their particular areas of interest that could be harnessed and what training needs do they have? Leaders also need to consider the training needs of the setting and decide which staff members are best placed to complete any training. This is so that the staffing is as knowledgeable and skilled as possible in order to achieve the very best outcomes for children.

The performance management program will also be used to address any underperformance of staff. Initially, staff must be supported to improve their performance through training, mentoring by more experienced or skilled staff and training. Staff must be very clear about what they need to do to improve, what success would look like for them and when this needs to be achieved. Failure to make the necessary improvements in the given time and with reasonable support in place may lead to dismissal. This is something that any leader would wish to avoid. However, children only have one chance at their education and cannot have this compromised because staff members are not performing at the level they should be. Highly effective leaders do not accept what is unacceptable.

Professional development: The most effective leaders understand how important it is to invest in staff training and development. They find the time and resource to ensure that all staff members have an entitlement to a training and development programme. Leaders ask themselves four crucial points when creating a training plan:

- What skills or knowledge does the setting lack? What do we need to have within the setting in order to improve?
- How can I support particular interests and passions of staff so that they feel professionally stimulated whilst remaining enthusiastic about their role?
- Do we have staff members that need to raise their qualification levels to improve practice and outcomes for children? How can we support this?
- What is the succession plan for leadership within the setting? Have potential future leaders been identified and how are we helping them to develop their leadership?

Alongside a programme of personalised professional development, the best leaders organise training and briefing sessions to constantly remind all staff members about expectations, protocols and best practice. In this way, staff members are reminded of what is expected of them and are able to keep abreast of national initiatives that may impact on their practice. They can discuss, as a whole team, how best to respond to new initiatives and ideas. Whole staff training sessions should also allow time for reflection about one's own personal practice and effectiveness as well as that of the team. Such insights feed into the cycle of self-evaluation.

Staff very much appreciate this opportunity to be consulted and are pleased their opinions matter. People will always work hard to ensure success if they feel they have played an important role in shaping practice.

Planning for improvement:

Although staff development is a personal matter which may differ from setting to setting, it is true to say that there are certain aspects of provision that are typically delivered less effectively than others. It may therefore be wise for leaders to consider some of the following as starting points for improvement:

- How would you judge the quality of all adult interaction with children? This has the greatest impact on children's learning.
- Does the setting prioritise children's communication and language skills, personal social and emotional development, mathematics and early literacy? Is it clear from planning that these are prioritised?
- Does the setting support parents in understanding and helping a child's development in the aforementioned areas?
- Do staff use their knowledge of what children can and cannot do, do or do

not understand to adjust planning and activities to carefully meet the needs of individual children and groups, particularly those who are most at risk of falling behind?

- Are regular, explicit teaching opportunities planned for all children?
- Do staff members take every opportunity available to extend children's learning, introduce and model new vocabulary and language? Is this then applied in different contexts and different times so that children become confident in its use?
- Are children engaged in rich, stimulating and exciting activities that encourages talk and language acquisition?
- Do staff members ask open-ended questions that require extended answers and challenge a child's thinking?
- Do staff members listen carefully to children and know when it is best to intervene and when it is best to leave them to their own devices?

Families

The most effective practice promotes a strong partnership with parents and carers so that all adults involved with children can work together to secure the best outcomes for them. Wise leaders nurture and build relationships, even before a child starts at a setting. When communicating with parents, you have to remember that for many this will be the first time their child has had any independent interaction with other people, away from home. If you have a difficult message to share with them, this must be done delicately and with a sense of perspective, it may be the first time they have ever heard anything negative about their child. At all times, positive relationships must be maintained with parents and carers.

As a leader, do you ensure parents and carers are given the information they want and need? Typically, this sort of information would include:

- How the child is socialising with other children and adults
- How they are developing socially, physically and academically, compared to their peers and their starting point
- The child's strengths and interests
- The things that the child finds more difficult and therefore needs to practice and rehearse at home
- Their emerging characteristics, are they shy, confident, caring and able to share and play with others? What can be done at home and within the setting to address any issues?

Communication should not be one way. As a leader, you need to consider:

- What systems have you put in place to ensure that parents and carers can talk

to you about any concerns or worries?
- How do you know that they are happy with provision that has been put in place for their child?
- Do you ask them how they think it could be improved?
- Do parents have the opportunity first thing in the morning to communicate any concerns or issues to you that might impact on the child's day?
- Do parents have the opportunity to regularly meet with key workers to talk about their child's development and progress?
- Do you lead opportunities to meet with parents in an informal way in order to build positive relationships before you might have to have any difficult conversations with them?

Compliance

Whilst much of this chapter has focused on staff development and the quality of teaching, it is also crucial that leaders are fully aware of all legislation and practice that they must be compliant with. Children's health and safety are of paramount importance and leaders must regularly audit the safety of their provision and their compliance with regulations. A number of documents are worthy of particular note, they include:

- Early years compliance handbook, Ofsted, September 2015
- Early years inspection handbook, Ofsted, September 2015
- Inspecting registered childcare providers, Ofsted, March 2015

All of these are readily available from the Ofsted website www.gov.uk/government/organisations/ofsted and will be regularly updated with any new requirements. Leaders must invest time in regularly looking at any updated documents to check that their setting is fully compliant with the latest expectation.

Finally, in summary, is a list of the characteristics of highly effective leadership in early years setting. You should ask yourself, whilst reading through the list:

How many of the following are true for your setting?

How many do you need to develop further?

The golden rules of highly effective leadership in early years settings

- There is a clear vision for the setting that is fully understood by all who are involved. Staff members do not just articulate this but they 'live' it, each and every day.

- Leaders never lose sight of the fact that their most important focus must always be the quality of teaching and what they need to do to ensure this is improved or sustained at the very highest level.
- Leadership is distributed and not reliant on any one person. All staff members must feel empowered to contribute to improvement.
- The setting has a culture of high expectations both of staff and of the children.
- Leaders lead by example; they do not ask any staff member to do something they could not or would not do themselves.
- Leaders give themselves time to sit and reflect on practice within their setting as well as local and national initiatives. They use these reflections to improve their provision.
- Leaders must ensure that all staff members follow policy and protocol.
- Leaders are relentless in ensuring consistency and high standards are maintained. They do not accept what is unacceptable.
- Decisions are only ever made in the best interest of the children; they are never made in the best interests of the staff.
- Leaders know that they are servants of their community, without the children and their families there would be no setting. They remember this when dealing with children and families, treating them with great respect.
- Regardless of a child's starting points, leaders ensure that all children make good progress and achieve well. Where there are gaps in the child's understanding or acquisition of skills, the curriculum is planned to compensate for this and address any underperformance.
- Leaders regularly review the curriculum to ensure that it is broad, balanced and rich. Activities that children engage in are never mundane but stimulating, encouraging children to discuss and engage.
- Leaders in the setting act as quality control monitors. They check the quality of planning, delivery, the environment, engagement and the accuracy of staff assessments.

References:

Cook, J. (2013): *Leadership and Management in the Early Years.* Practical Pre-School Books.

Department for Education. (2014): *Statutory framework for the Early Years Foundation Stage.* Gov.uk.

Early Years Matters (2014): *Leadership.* Earlyyearsmatters.co.uk.

Lewis, J. Hill, J. (2012): *What does leadership look like in early childhood settings?* Every Child Magazine, Early Childhood Australia.

Ofsted (2013): *Achieving and maintaining high-quality early years provision: Getting it right the first time.* Gov.uk.

Ofsted (2008): *Early years: Leading to excellence.* Department for Education.

Ofsted. (2013): *Getting it right first time: Achieving and maintaining high quality early years provision.* Gov.uk.

Robb, S. (2015): *Leading and early years setting.* Teach Early Years.

Siraj-Blatchford, I. Wah Sum, C. (2013): *Understanding and advancing systems leadership in the early years.* National College for Teaching and Leadership.

Sharp, C. Lord, P. Handscomb, G. Macleod, S. Southcott, C. George, N, and Jeffes, J. (2012): *Highly effective leadership in children's centres.* National College for School Leadership.

Inspecting the early years

All those who work in early years settings, whether they are leaders, teachers or early years practitioners, need to ensure that they have a very good understanding of the most up to date Ofsted framework. This framework will be used to form judgements about how successful their setting is. Staff members need to be completely familiar with the minimum expectations and the grade descriptors for good and outstanding practice.

This familiarity needs to lead to changes and improvements being made in the setting to fulfil the higher criteria, which are laid out very specifically. Those who lead and manage the setting should not underestimate the positive impact of being judged good or better and the negative impact of receiving judgements that show the setting to be less than good. What parent would place their child in a setting that Ofsted have judged to be not good enough? What staff member would happily remain working in such a place?

Ofsted's early years inspection handbook provides an excellent resource for leaders and practitioners to use to compare their own practice to what is nationally agreed as good and outstanding. Inspectors will make judgements about the following key areas of provision:

- Overall effectiveness
- Effectiveness of leadership and management
- Quality of teaching, learning and assessment
- Personal development, behaviour and welfare
- Outcomes for the children

Under each of these headings in the handbook, you will find a set of criteria that demonstrates what inspectors will be focusing on and what excellent provision might include. Whilst these bullet points are not to be treated as a checklist, they offer leaders an insight into the sorts of areas they should be focusing on and hint at what excellent provision may look like. It would be prudent then, given that Ofsted has explicitly identified its areas of focus, for all leaders to reflect on the effectiveness of their own practice with regard to these key areas.

Self-evaluation

All settings should regularly evaluate their practice and use Ofsted's grade characteristics to form the basis of a self-evaluation form. This is an excellent place to start and will ensure that leaders are focusing on the appropriate areas. Whilst Ofsted are very clear that they do not expect any particular format or style of self-evaluation, it can only help if your self-evaluation is using a similar format, criteria and language as that which is contained within the Ofsted handbook. There is no expectation that self-evaluation needs to be a weighty tome. On the contrary, it needs to provide a short, readable narrative which tells the story of the school context, where the setting currently is in terms of the five key areas of provision, its strengths and the specific things that the setting needs to do to improve. It may be useful to consider the following format as a starting point for self-evaluation.

<table>
<tr><td colspan="4">Name of setting</td></tr>
<tr><td>Section</td><td colspan="3">Summary Evaluation</td></tr>
<tr><td>School context</td><td colspan="3">Include data about your setting that you consider important (% FSM /PP / EAL / SEN/More able, deprivation indicator etc.)
Is there anything about your locality or community that you consider important?
Stability/experience of staff
Mobility of pupils/attendance levels</td></tr>
<tr><td rowspan="2">Priorities for the current development plan
What is the setting currently focusing on to improve?
This information will help inspectors decide on how capable leaders are. Have they identified the right things as priorities for improvement?</td><td>Achievement/outcomes for children:</td><td>Quality of teaching, learning and assessment:</td><td>Personal development, behaviour and welfare:</td></tr>
<tr><td>Effectiveness of Leadership & management:</td><td>Community:</td><td>Environment:</td></tr>
<tr><td rowspan="2">Progress made by the setting against areas for improvement identified in the last inspection
Has the setting acted on the advice that was previously given?</td><td>Key issue:</td><td>Progress made:</td><td>Next steps:</td></tr>
<tr><td>Take this information from your last inspection report</td><td></td><td></td></tr>
</table>

<table>
<tr><th>Effectiveness of leadership and management</th><th>Strengths:</th><th>Areas for development:</th></tr>
<tr><td>GRADE:
Impact of leaders at all levels, including governors and how well they pursue excellence and demonstrate an ambitious vision; well focused improvement plan and robust self-evaluation; monitoring and evaluation; use of assessment information; taking account of the views of parents and children; provides an appropriate broad and balanced curriculum; actively promote equality and diversity, tackling poor behaviour and narrowing any gaps in outcomes between different groups of children; actively promotes British values; safeguarding arrangements are effective – including promoting welfare and preventing radicalisation and extremism
(see also page 31 -34 of early years inspection handbook)</td><td></td><td></td></tr>
<tr><td>Evidence base</td><td colspan="2">How do you know?
What evidence have you used, including that from independent advisers and consultants, to form your judgement? List and include any reports and data as appendices.
Where can this evidence be found? Signpost to other documents and appendices. List these.</td></tr>
<tr><th>Quality of teaching, learning and assessment</th><th>Strengths:</th><th>Areas for development:</th></tr>
<tr><td>GRADE:
High expectations consistently demonstrated including for most able and disadvantaged; staff have secure understanding of the age group they are working with and have relevant subject knowledge; assessment information is gathered and used to support progress. It is informed by children's parents in previous providers as appropriate; assessment is used to identify children who are falling behind and may need additional support and ensures all children make good progress and achieve well; children understand how to develop as result of regular interaction and encouragement from staff; information given by the school to parents helps them understand how the children are doing and what they need to do to progress; equality of opportunity is promoted through teaching and learning
(See also page 34-38 of early years inspection handbook)</td><td></td><td></td></tr>
<tr><td>Evidence base</td><td colspan="2">How do you know?
What evidence have you used, including that from independent advisers and consultants, to form your judgement? List and include any reports and data as appendices.
Where can this evidence be found? Signpost to other documents and appendices. List these.</td></tr>
</table>

Personal development, behaviour and welfare	Strengths:	Areas for development:
GRADE: *There is a positive culture across the whole setting; children are self-confident and understand how to be successful; they enjoy their learning, develop independence and use their imagination; social and emotional preparation for the transition within the setting or to another setting is highly effective; children feel emotionally secure through attachments with practitioners; attendance is prompt and regular; children follow the guidance on behaviour and conduct and interact well with each other.* *(See also page 38-41 of the early years inspection handbook)*		
Evidence base	*How do you know?* *What evidence have you used (including that from independent advisers and consultants) to form your judgement? List and include any reports and data as appendices* *Where can this evidence be found? Signpost to other documents and appendices. List these.*	
Outcomes for children	**Strengths:**	**Areas for development:**
GRADE: *All children progress well from different starting points; once children meet or exceed the level of development that is typical for their age they can move onto the next stage of their education.* *(See also page 41-44 of the early years inspection handbook)*		
Evidence base *Not just end of key stage but baseline/entry data, as well as in year progress cohort data (including cohort subgroups). In particular, how do your Pupil Premium pupils get on compared to non-PP?*	*How do you know?* *What evidence have you used, including that from independent advisers and consultants, to form your judgement? List and include any reports and data as appendices* *Where can this evidence be found? Signpost to other documents and appendices. List these.*	

How to grade your setting as part of a self-evaluation exercise

A useful exercise to complete as a leadership team, or indeed as a whole staff activity, is to look at the grade descriptors for each of the Ofsted key areas and decide which one offers the best fit for your setting. You can do this by highlighting elements within each descriptor that you feel you can confidently say are firmly established at your setting. When you then ask 'how do I know?' you are able to evidence your judgement using data and reports that have been either externally generated or, if internally generated, were moderated externally. This greatly adds to the reliability of any evidence offered.

Example:

Grade descriptors for personal development, behaviour and welfare	**Evidence** **How do you know?**	**Next steps to improve the setting**
Outstanding (1) • The highly stimulating environment and wide range of activities ensure that children are highly motivated and very eager to join in. They consistently show the characteristics of effective learning. They show high levels of curiosity, imagination and concentration. Older children listen intently and are highly responsive to adults and each other. • Children's health, welfare and wellbeing are significantly enhanced by the vigilant and highly consistent implementation of robust policies, procedures and practice. High standards of care and hygiene practice support the personal care needs of babies and toddlers. • Practitioners are highly skilled and sensitive in helping children of all ages form secure emotional attachments. This gives children a strong base for developing their independence to explore their world and increases their confidence in their own abilities. • Children increasingly show high levels of confidence in social situations. They develop a positive sense of themselves and their place in the world. They develop a very good understanding of how to keep themselves safe and how to manage risks and challenges. • The strong skills of all key persons ensure that all children are emotionally well prepared for the next stages in their learning. Practitioners skilfully support children's transitions both within the setting and to other settings and prepare them for the move to school. • Children demonstrate exceptionally positive behaviour and high levels of self-control, cooperation and respect for others that are appropriate for their age. They do not distract others or become distracted themselves. • Children's welfare and personal development are central to everything practitioners do. They are very effective in supporting children's growing understanding of how to keep themselves safe and healthy. Practitioners give children a wide range of experiences that promote understanding of people, families and communities beyond their own. They teach children the language of feelings and give them opportunities to reflect on their differences.		

Good (2) • Practitioners provide a stimulating, welcoming environment, both indoors and out, that keeps children motivated and interested in a broad range of activities. Children are keen learners who regularly display the characteristics of effective learning. They listen carefully to adults and each other. • A well-established key person system helps children form secure attachments and promotes their well-being and independence. Relationships between staff and babies are sensitive, stimulating and responsive. • Practitioners adhere consistently to agreed strategies to promote good behaviour and regular attendance. They provide clear guidance for children about what is and is not acceptable behaviour. • Practitioners help children to become independent in managing their own personal needs. • Key persons ensure children are emotionally well prepared for the next stages in their learning. • Children's good behaviour shows that they feel safe. They gain an understanding of risk through activities that encourage them to explore their environment. • Practitioners give clear messages to children about why it is important to have a healthy diet and the need for physical exercise while providing these things within the setting. Children are learning to respect and celebrate each other's differences. They develop an understanding of diversity beyond their immediate family experience through a range of activities that teach them effectively about people in the wider world.		
Requires improvement (3) • Provision to support children's personal development, behaviour and welfare is not yet good. Any breaches of the statutory requirements for safeguarding and welfare and/or learning and development do not have a significant impact on children's safety, well-being and personal development.		

Inadequate (4) **Personal development, behaviour and welfare are likely to be inadequate if one or more of the following applies.** • Breaches of the statutory requirements for safeguarding and welfare and/or learning and development have a significant impact on children's safety, well-being and personal development. • Practitioners do not support children's social and emotional well-being and prepare them for transitions within the setting and/or to other settings and school. • The key person system does not work effectively to support children's emotional well-being and so some children fail to form secure attachments with their carers. Babies are not stimulated. • Children's behaviour is not managed consistently. As a result, more than occasionally, their lack of engagement in activities and/or poor behaviour leads to a disorderly environment that hinders children's learning and/or puts them and others at risk. • Not all practitioners have sufficient knowledge and/or they are not vigilant enough to ensure that children are kept safe and that their health and welfare are promoted. This means children do not know, relative to their ages, how to keep themselves safe and healthy. • Children have a narrow experience that does not promote their understanding of people and communities beyond their own or help them to recognise and accept each other's differences.		

From the above example, it is clear that the best fit is grade 2, 'Good'. In addition this exercise demonstrates what is not securely in place and therefore what the setting should focus on in order to improve.

Task:

Start from the bottom i.e. the grade descriptors for inadequate, to make sure that you have not missed any key descriptor that could be significant and have a detrimental effect on children in your setting or on an inspection outcome. Work your way up from 'requires improvement' to good' and 'outstanding'. By highlighting the descriptors that you can confidently say are firmly established in your setting, you will necessarily identify what is not. In this way you will be able to see your best fit in terms of the descriptors and more importantly, you will have identified the areas you need to focus on in order to secure improvement.

Safeguarding

This is an area of inspection that rightly has a huge emphasis. Whilst there is no separate grade given for safeguarding, inspectors will always make a written judgement about safeguarding in the leadership and management section of a report.

Leaders should make themselves familiar with the following publications, which can be found on the gov.uk website:

- 'Inspecting safeguarding early years, education and skills settings' (June 2015)
- 'Working together to safeguard children' (March 2015)

We have dedicated an entire chapter to safeguarding in this book, it is crucial that all leaders within early years settings take careful account of the recommendations and minimum expectations of safeguarding in early years as any failure to meet statutory requirements will reflect badly on the setting and may lead to an inspector judging the setting to be inadequate and further, recommending that Ofsted issue a 'welfare requirements notice' detailing issues that need to be addressed immediately, as part of the written report.

Managing your inspection

The outcome of any inspection will undoubtedly be shaped by the way in which leaders within the setting manage the process. It is therefore crucial then that leaders understand and manage this before, during and after the process is complete.

Before the inspection

Ensure that the leadership team, including governors, have completed some form of self-evaluation and understand the strengths and weaknesses of the setting. Do all leaders demonstrate consistency in what they are saying?

There is certainly no expectation, but it may be helpful to provide inspectors with information about the character of each cohort/class/room they will be visiting in terms of staff experience, pupil abilities, children in receipt of pupil premium and SEN, EAL and more able pupils.

Ensure that all rooms are clearly labelled so that there is no confusion when inspectors, who are unfamiliar with the setting, move around and visit rooms. Particularly for larger settings, make sure to identify a room or space where the inspector/s can keep their belongings and hold meetings.

One place inspectors will go to in order to gain an initial view of a setting is the website. Is your website fully compliant in terms of offering the information it should do? For schools, the gov.uk site regularly updates information regarding what maintained schools must publish online. It would be prudent to visit this site and ensure that the information you publish complies with the expectations.

If you read through the inspection handbook, you will see that there are a number of activities that inspectors must complete in order to gather information and evidence.

The inspector must track the experiences and development levels of representative sample of children; they will track at least two children. Whilst it is at the inspector's own discretion to decide who they will track, it may be helpful and prudent to have already completed some case studies; particularly ensure you include the children who are eligible for the early years pupil premium.

Case studies should include the following:

- An individual assessment that demonstrate the practitioners' knowledge of the child.
- The progress check for any child aged two.
- The impact of any early years pupil premium funding on the child's progress.
- Copies of records of discussions held with each child's key person and information about progress.
- Copies of records to show the child's progress is tracked, including any concerns raised and subsequent action taken.
- Any information on whether the child is developing skills ready for the next stage of education.

For child minders with small numbers of children, inspectors will not be able to look at a sample, however case study information will be equally valuable.

During an inspection, inspectors are charged with completing a number of essential activities to help them gather evidence and form a view. Given this is the case, it would be prudent for leaders to use the same such activities as part of their regular and on-going evaluation of the setting. Inspection will go much more smoothly if staff members are familiar with and used to being involved in such activities as:

- Observation of staff and their interaction with children
- Dialogue with staff and children: what do conversations with children tell you about their learning and the effectiveness of the setting?
- Joint observations: do you regularly ask staff to share their findings and evaluations?
- Regular discussion with staff about their attainment and progress data for children: do they talk with knowledge and insight about the needs of individuals in their care?
- Book/work scrutiny: is there evidence of appropriate progress being made for all groups? Are policies and practices applied consistently across all groups/ rooms?
- Have you evidence that you regularly meet with parents to seek their views? Do you then act on these?
- Discussing and identifying the professional development needs of staff: how does staff training impact on the outcomes of the children?

During the inspection

The inspection process provides leaders with the opportunity to work alongside an independent professional colleague, identifying strengths and weaknesses and judging the setting against a set of national criteria. Inspectors hold a mirror to the setting. For effective leaders there will be no surprises, because of their rigorous self-assessment they will already know the strengths and weaknesses of their setting.

Providers will be offered the opportunity to work alongside inspectors, making joint observations and being involved in all meetings. Whilst there is no obligation to participate, gone are the days when inspections were 'done to' providers. The best leaders are keen to contribute and welcome this opportunity to share information, challenge any misunderstanding and shape the final judgements.

It is quite right that leaders should offer some level of challenge to any judgements they feel are inaccurate. Inspectors are in settings for such a limited amount of time that the expert knowledge of providers is invaluable to them and the inspection process. Do not feel that it is disrespectful to challenge any hypotheses that are being formulated. Quite the contrary, if it is done in the right way then challenge serves to demonstrate strength of leadership and a secure understanding of the setting.

Do not be frightened to ask questions or ask inspectors to consider additional information that you feel may be pertinent. Inspectors want to do a good job and want to tell a true and accurate story of the setting. As long as it is timely, inspectors will be happy to look at any additional information that school leaders feel is relevant.

On rare occasions, leaders may have concerns about an inspection visit. If this happens, issues must be raised with the inspector as soon as possible whilst the inspection is taking place. This provides the opportunity to resolve issues before the inspection is completed.

After the inspection

Use the report as the basis of your next development plan. Recommendations made specifically focus on what a setting needs to do to improve and so must be acted upon swiftly. This is not just in order to get a better report next time but, more importantly, because it will improve the provision, experiences and outcomes for the children in your care.

References:

Department for Education (2013): *Early years outcomes: A non-statutory guide for practitioners and inspectors to help inform understanding of child development through the early years.* Foundationyears.org.uk.

Ofsted. (2015): *Early years inspection handbook.* Gov.uk.

Ofsted. (2015): *Inspections of early years and childcare providers.* Gov.uk.

Ofsted. (2015): *Common Inspection Framework.* Gov.uk.

Ofsted. (2014): *Childcare Register Requirements: childcare providers on non-domestic or domestic premises: a childcare factsheet.* Gov.uk.

Ofsted (2015): *Inspecting safeguarding in early years, education and skills settings.* Gov.uk.

Ofsted (2015): *Early years compliance handbook.* Gov.uk.

Ofsted (2013): *Getting it right first time: achieving and maintaining high quality early years provision.* Gov.uk

Ofsted. (2014): *Reporting requirements for early years inspection.* Gov.uk.

Department for Education Early Years Outcomes 2013

A non-statutory guide for practitioners and inspectors to help inform understanding of child development through the early years.

The Early Years Foundation Stage (EYFS) requires early years practitioners to review children's progress and share a summary with parents at two points:

- between the ages of 24 and 36 months via the progress check; and
- at the end of reception via the EYFS profile.

This document is a non-statutory guide to support practitioners. It can be used by childminders, nurseries and others, such as Ofsted, throughout the early years as a guide to making best-fit judgements about whether a child is showing typical development for their age, may be at risk of delay or is ahead for their age.

1. Communication and language

The tables below set out what you should be observing a child doing at each stage, if they are developing typically for their age.

Listening and attention

Age	Typical behaviour
Birth to 11 months	Turns towards a familiar sound then locates range of sounds with accuracy. Listens to, distinguishes and responds to intonations and sounds of voices. Reacts in interaction with others by smiling, looking and moving. Quietens or alerts to the sound of speech. Looks intently at a person talking, but stops responding if speaker turns away. Listens to familiar sounds, words, or finger plays. Fleeting Attention – not under child's control, new stimuli takes whole attention.
8 to 20 months	Moves whole bodies to sounds they enjoy, such as music or a regular beat. Has a strong exploratory impulse. Concentrates intently on an object or activity of own choosing for short periods. Pays attention to dominant stimulus – easily distracted bynoises or other people talking.

16 to 26 months	Listens to and enjoys rhythmic patterns in rhymes and stories. Enjoys rhymes and demonstrates listening by trying to join in with actions or vocalisations. Rigid attention – may appear not to hear.
22 to 36 months	Listens with interest to the noises adults make when they read stories. Recognises and responds to many familiar sounds, e.g. turning to a knock on the door, looking at or going to the door. Shows interest in play with sounds, songs and rhymes. Single channelled attention. Can shift to a different task if attention fully obtained – using child's name helps focus.
30 to 50 months	Listens to others one to one or in small groups, when conversation interests them. Listens to stories with increasing attention and recall. Joins in with repeated refrains and anticipates key events and phrases in rhymes and stories. Focusing attention – still listen or do, but can shift own attention. Is able to follow directions (if not intently focused on own choice of activity).
40 to 60+ months	Maintains attention, concentrates and sits quietly during appropriate activity. Two-channelled attention – can listen and do for short span.

Early learning goal – listening and attention

Children listen attentively in a range of situations. They listen to stories, accurately anticipating key events and respond to what they hear with relevant comments, questions or actions. They give their attention to what others say and respond appropriately, while engaged in another activity.

Understanding

Age	Typical behaviour
Birth to 11 months	Stops and looks when hears own name. Starts to understand contextual clues, e.g. familiar gestures, words and sounds.
8 to 20 months	Developing the ability to follow others' body language, including pointing and gesture. Responds to the different things said when in a familiar context with a special person (e.g. 'Where's Mummy?', Where's your nose?'). Understanding of single words in context is developing, e.g. 'cup', 'milk', 'daddy'.
16 to 26 months	Selects familiar objects by name and will go and find objects when asked, or identify objects from a group. Understands simple sentences (e.g. 'Throw the ball'.)

22 to 36 months	Identifies action words by pointing to the right picture, e.g. "Who's jumping?" Understands more complex sentences, e.g. 'Put your toys away and then we'll read a book.' Understands 'who', 'what', 'where' in simple questions (e.g. who's that? What's that? Where is?). Developing understanding of simple concepts (e.g. big/little).
30 to 50 months	Understands use of objects (e.g. "What do we use to cut things?') Shows understanding of prepositions such as 'under', 'on 30 to 50 months top', 'behind' by carrying out an action or selecting correct picture. Responds to simple instructions, e.g. to get or put away an object. Beginning to understand 'why' and 'how' questions.
40 to 60+ months	Responds to instructions involving a two-part sequence. Understands humour, e.g. nonsense rhymes, jokes. Able to follow a story without pictures or props. Listens and responds to ideas expressed by others in conversation or discussion.

Early learning goal – understanding

Children follow instructions involving several ideas or actions. They answer 'how' and 'why' questions about their experiences and in response to stories or events.

Speaking

Age	Typical behaviour
Birth to 11 months	Communicates needs and feelings in a variety of ways including crying, gurgling, babbling and squealing. Makes own sounds in response when talked to by familiar adults. Lifts arms in anticipation of being picked up. Practises and gradually develops speech sounds (babbling) to communicate with adults; says sounds like 'baba, nono,
8 to 20 months	Uses sounds in play, e.g. 'brrrm' for toy car. Uses single words. Frequently imitates words and sounds. Enjoys babbling and increasingly experiments with using sounds and words to communicate for a range of purposes (e.g. teddy, more, no, bye-bye.) Uses pointing with eye gaze to make requests, and to share an interest. Creates personal words as they begin to develop language.

16 to 26 months	Copies familiar expressions, e.g. 'Oh dear', 'All gone'. Beginning to put two words together (e.g. 'want ball', 'more juice'). Uses different types of everyday words (nouns, verbs and adjectives, e.g. banana, go, sleep, hot). Beginning to ask simple questions. Beginning to talk about people and things that are not present.
22 to 36 months	Uses language as a powerful means of widening contacts, sharing feelings, experiences and thoughts. Holds a conversation, jumping from topic to topic. Learns new words very rapidly and is able to use them in communicating. Uses gestures, sometimes with limited talk, e.g. reaches towards toy, saying 'I have it'. Uses a variety of questions (e.g. what, where, who). Uses simple sentences (e.g.' Mummy gonna work.') Beginning to use word endings (e.g. going, cats).
30 to 50 months	Beginning to use more complex sentences to link thoughts (e.g. using and, because). Can retell a simple past event in correct order (e.g. went down slide, hurt finger). Uses talk to connect ideas, explain what is happening and anticipate what might happen next, recall and relive past experiences. Questions why things happen and gives explanations. Asks e.g. who, what, when, how. Uses a range of tenses (e.g. play, playing, will play, played). Uses intonation, rhythm and phrasing to make the meaning clear to others. Uses vocabulary focused on objects and people that are of particular importance to them. Builds up vocabulary that reflects the breadth of their experiences. Uses talk in pretending that objects stand for something else
40 to 60+ months	Extends vocabulary, especially by grouping and naming, exploring the meaning and sounds of new words. Uses language to imagine and recreate roles and experiences in play situations. Links statements and sticks to a main theme or intention. Uses talk to organise, sequence and clarify thinking, ideas, feelings and events. Introduces a storyline or narrative into their play.

Early learning goal – speaking

Children express themselves effectively, showing awareness of listeners' needs. They use past, present and future forms accurately when talking about events that have happened or are to happen in the future. They develop their own narratives and explanations by connecting ideas or events.

2. Physical development

The tables below set out what you should be observing a child doing at each stage, if they are developing typically for their age.

Moving and handling

Age	Typical behaviour
Birth to 11 months	Turns head in response to sounds and sights. Gradually develops ability to hold up own head. Makes movements with arms and legs which gradually become more controlled. Rolls over from front to back, from back to front. When lying on tummy becomes able to lift first head and then chest, supporting self with forearms and then straight arms. Watches and explores hands and feet, e.g. when lying on back lifts legs into vertical position and grasps feet. Reaches out for, touches and begins to hold objects. Explores objects with mouth, often picking up an object and holding it to the mouth.
8 to 20 months	Sits unsupported on the floor. When sitting, can lean forward to pick up small toys. Pulls to standing, holding on to furniture or person for support. Crawls, bottom shuffles or rolls continuously to move around. Walks around furniture lifting one foot and stepping sideways (cruising), and walks with one or both hands held by adult. Takes first few steps independently. Passes toys from one hand to the other. Holds an object in each hand and brings them together in the middle, e.g. holds two blocks and bangs them together. Picks up small objects between thumb and fingers. Enjoys the sensory experience of making marks in damp sand, paste or paint. Holds pen or crayon using a whole hand (palmar) grasp and makes random marks with different strokes.
16 to 26 months	Walks upstairs holding hand of adult. Comes downstairs backwards on knees (crawling). Beginning to balance blocks to build a small tower. Makes connections between their movement and the marks they make.

22 to 36 months	Runs safely on whole foot. Squats with steadiness to rest or play with object on the ground, and rises to feet without using hands. Climbs confidently and is beginning to pull themselves up on nursery play climbing equipment. Can kick a large ball. Turns pages in a book, sometimes several at once. Shows control in holding and using jugs to pour, hammers, books and mark-making tools. Beginning to use three fingers (tripod grip) to hold writing tools. Imitates drawing simple shapes such as circles and lines. Walks upstairs or downstairs holding onto a rail two feet to a step. May be beginning to show preference for dominant hand.
30 to 50 months	Moves freely and with pleasure and confidence in a range of ways, such as slithering, shuffling, rolling, crawling, walking, running, jumping, skipping, sliding and hopping. Mounts stairs, steps or climbing equipment using alternate feet. Walks downstairs, two feet to each step while carrying a small object. Runs skilfully and negotiates space successfully, adjusting speed or direction to avoid obstacles. Can stand momentarily on one foot when shown. Can catch a large ball. Draws lines and circles using gross motor movements. Uses one-handed tools and equipment, e.g. makes snips in paper with child scissors. Holds pencil between thumb and two fingers, no longer using whole-hand grasp. Holds pencil near point between first two fingers and thumb and uses it with good control. Can copy some letters, e.g. letters from their name.
40 to 60+ months	Experiments with different ways of moving. Jumps off an object and lands appropriately. Negotiates space successfully when playing racing and chasing games with other children, adjusting speed or changing direction to avoid obstacles. Travels with confidence and skill around, under, over and through balancing and climbing equipment. Shows increasing control over an object in pushing, patting, throwing, catching or kicking it. Uses simple tools to effect changes to materials. Handles tools, objects, construction and malleable materials safely and with increasing control. Shows a preference for a dominant hand. Begins to use anticlockwise movement and retrace vertical lines. Begins to form recognisable letters. Uses a pencil and holds it effectively to form recognisable letters, most of which are correctly formed.

Early learning goal – moving and handling

Children show good control and co-ordination in large and small movements. They move confidently in a range of ways, safely negotiating space. They handle equipment and tools effectively, including pencils for writing.

Health and self-care

Age	Typical behaviour
Birth to 11 months	Responds to and thrives on warm, sensitive physical contact and care. Expresses discomfort, hunger or thirst. Anticipates food routines with interest.
8 to 20 months	Opens mouth for spoon. Holds own bottle or cup. Grasps finger foods and brings them to mouth. Attempts to use spoon: can guide towards mouth but food often falls off. Can actively cooperate with nappy changing (lies still, helps hold legs up). Starts to communicate urination, bowel movement.
16 to 26 months	Develops own likes and dislikes in food and drink. Willing to try new food textures and tastes. Holds cup with both hands and drinks without much spilling. Clearly communicates wet or soiled nappy or pants. Shows some awareness of bladder and bowel urges. Shows awareness of what a potty or toilet is used for. Shows a desire to help with dressing/undressing and hygiene routines.
22 to 36 months	Feeds self competently with spoon. Drinks well without spilling. Clearly communicates their need for potty or toilet. Beginning to recognise danger and seeks support of significant adults for help. Helps with clothing, e.g. puts on hat, unzips zipper on jacket, takes off unbuttoned shirt. Beginning to be independent in self-care, but still often needs adult support.

30 to 50 months	Can tell adults when hungry or tired or when they want to rest or play. Observes the effects of activity on their bodies. Understands that equipment and tools have to be used safely. Gains more bowel and bladder control and can attend to toileting needs most of the time themselves. Can usually manage washing and drying hands. Dresses with help, e.g. puts arms into open-fronted coat or shirt when held up, pulls up own trousers, and pulls up zipper once it is fastened at the bottom.
40 to 60+ months	Eats a healthy range of foodstuffs and understands need for variety in food. Usually dry and clean during the day. Shows some understanding that good practices with regard to exercise, eating, sleeping and hygiene can contribute to good health. Shows understanding of the need for safety when tackling new challenges, and considers and manages some risks. Shows understanding of how to transport and store equipment safely. Practices some appropriate safety measures without direct

Early learning goal – health and self-care

Children know the importance for good health of physical exercise, and a healthy diet, and talk about ways to keep healthy and safe. They manage their own basic hygiene and personal needs successfully, including dressing and going to the toilet independently.

3. Personal, social and emotional development

The tables below set out what you should be observing a child doing at each stage, if they are developing typically for their age.

Self-confidence and self-awareness

Age	Typical behaviour
Birth to 11 months	Laughs and gurgles, e.g. shows pleasure at being tickled and other physical interactions. Uses voice, gesture, eye contact and facial expression to make contact with people and keep their attention.
8 to 20 months	Enjoys finding own nose, eyes or tummy as part of naming games. Learns that own voice and actions have effects on others. Uses pointing with eye gaze to make requests, and to share an interest. Engages other person to help achieve a goal, e.g. to get an object out of reach.

16 to 26 months	Explores new toys and environments, but 'checks in' regularly with familiar adult as and when needed. Gradually able to engage in pretend play with toys (supports child to understand their own thinking may be different from others). Demonstrates sense of self as an individual, e.g. wants to do things independently, says "No" to adult.
22 to 36 months	Separates from main carer with support and encouragement from a familiar adult. Expresses own preferences and interests.
30 to 50 months	Can select and use activities and resources with help. Welcomes and values praise for what they have done. Enjoys responsibility of carrying out small tasks. Is more outgoing towards unfamiliar people and more confident in new social situations. Confident to talk to other children when playing, and will communicate freely about own home and community. Shows confidence in asking adults for help.
40 to 60+ months	Confident to speak to others about own needs, wants, interests and opinions. Can describe self in positive terms and talk about abilities.

Early learning goal – self-confidence and self-awareness

Children are confident to try new activities, and say why they like some activities more than others. They are confident to speak in a familiar group, will talk about their ideas, and will choose the resources they need for their chosen activities. They say when they do or don't need help.

Managing feelings and behaviour

Age	Typical behaviour
Birth to 11 months	Is comforted by touch and people's faces and voices. Seeks physical and emotional comfort by snuggling into trusted adults. Calms from being upset when held, rocked, spoken or sung to with soothing voice. Shows a range of emotions such as pleasure, fear and excitement. Reacts emotionally to other people's emotions, e.g. smiles when smiled at and becomes distressed if hears another child crying.
8 to 20 months	Uses familiar adult to share feelings such as excitement or pleasure, and for 'emotional refuelling' when feeling tired, stressed or frustrated. Growing ability to soothe themselves, and may like to use a comfort object. Cooperates with caregiving experiences, e.g. dressing. Beginning to understand 'yes', 'no' and some boundaries.

16 to 26 months	Is aware of others' feelings, for example, looks concerned if hears crying or looks excited if hears a familiar happy voice. Growing sense of will and determination may result in feelings of anger and frustration which are difficult to handle, e.g. may have tantrums. Responds to a few appropriate boundaries, with encouragement and support. Begins to learn that some things are theirs, some things are shared, and some things belong to other people.
22 to 36 months	Seeks comfort from familiar adults when needed. Can express their own feelings such as sad, happy, cross, scared, worried. Responds to the feelings and wishes of others. Aware that some actions can hurt or harm others. Tries to help or give comfort when others are distressed. Shows understanding and cooperates with some boundaries and routines. Can inhibit own actions/behaviours, e.g. stop themselves from doing something they shouldn't do. Growing ability to distract self when upset, e.g. by engaging in a new play activity.
30 to 50 months	Aware of own feelings, and knows that some actions and words can hurt others' feelings. Begins to accept the needs of others and can take turns and share resources, sometimes with support from others. Can usually tolerate delay when needs are not immediately met, and understands wishes may not always be met. Can usually adapt behaviour to different events, social situations and changes in routine.
40 to 60+ months	Understands that own actions affect other people, for example, becomes upset or tries to comfort another child when they realise they have upset them. Aware of the boundaries set, and of behavioural expectations in the setting. Beginning to be able to negotiate and solve problems without aggression, e.g. when someone has taken their toy.

Early learning goal – managing feelings and behaviour

Children talk about how they and others show feelings, talk about their own and others' behaviour, and its consequences, and know that some behaviour is unacceptable. They work as part of a group or class, and understand and follow the rules. They adjust their behaviour to different situations, and take changes of routine in their stride.

Making relationships

Age	Typical behaviour
Birth to 11 months	Enjoys the company of others and seeks contact with others from birth. Gazes at faces and copies facial movements, e.g. sticking out tongue, opening mouth and widening eyes. Responds when talked to, for example, moves arms and legs, changes facial expression, moves body and makes mouth movements. Recognises and is most responsive to main carer's voice: face brightens, activity increases when familiar carer appears. Responds to what carer is paying attention to, e.g. following their gaze. Likes cuddles and being held: calms, snuggles in, smiles, gazes at carer's face or strokes carer's skin..
8 to 20 months	Seeks to gain attention in a variety of ways, drawing others into social interaction. Builds relationships with special people. Is wary of unfamiliar people. Interacts with others and explores new situations when supported by familiar person. Shows interest in the activities of others and responds differently to children and adults, e.g. may be more interested in watching children than adults or may pay more attention when children talk to them.
16 to 26 months	Plays alongside others. Uses a familiar adult as a secure base from which to explore independently in new environments, e.g. ventures away to play and interact with others, but returns for a cuddle or reassurance if becomes anxious. Plays cooperatively with a familiar adult, e.g. rolling a ball back and forth.
22 to 36 months	Interested in others' play and starting to join in. Seeks out others to share experiences. Shows affection and concern for people who are special to them. May form a special friendship with another child.
30 to 50 months	Can play in a group, extending and elaborating play ideas, e.g. building up a role-play activity with other children. Initiates play, offering cues to peers to join them. Keeps play going by responding to what others are saying or doing. Demonstrates friendly behaviour, initiating conversations and forming good relationships with peers and familiar adults..
40 to 60+ months	Initiates conversations, attends to and takes account of what others say. Explains own knowledge and understanding, and asks appropriate questions of others. Takes steps to resolve conflicts with other children, e.g. finding a compromise.

Early learning goal – making relationships

Children play co-operatively, taking turns with others. They take account of one another's ideas about how to organise their activity. They show sensitivity to others' needs and feelings, and form positive relationships with adults and other children.

4. Literacy

The tables below set out what you should be observing a child doing at each stage, if they are developing typically for their age.

Reading

Age	Typical behaviour
Birth to 11 months	Enjoys looking at books and other printed material with familiar people.
8 to 20 months	Handles books and printed material with interest.
16 to 26 months	Interested in books and rhymes and may have favourites.
22 to 36 months	Has some favourite stories, rhymes, songs, poems or jingles. Repeats words or phrases from familiar stories. Fills in the missing word or phrase in a known rhyme, story or game, e.g. 'Humpty Dumpty sat on a ...'.
30 to 50 months	Enjoys rhyming and rhythmic activities. Shows awareness of rhyme and alliteration. Recognises rhythm in spoken words. Listens to and joins in with stories and poems, one-to-one and also in small groups. Joins in with repeated refrains and anticipates key events and phrases in rhymes and stories. Beginning to be aware of the way stories are structured. Suggests how the story might end. Listens to stories with increasing attention and recall. Describes main story settings, events and principal characters. Shows interest in illustrations and print in books and print in the environment. Recognises familiar words and signs such as own name and advertising logos. Looks at books independently. Handles books carefully. Knows information can be relayed in the form of print. Holds books the correct way up and turns pages. Knows that print carries meaning and, in English, is readfrom left to right and top to bottom.

40 to 60+ months	Continues a rhyming string. Hears and says the initial sound in words. Can segment the sounds in simple words and blend them together and knows which letters represent some of them. Links sounds to letters, naming and sounding the letters of the alphabet. Begins to read words and simple sentences. Uses vocabulary and forms of speech that are increasingly influenced by their experiences of books. Enjoys an increasing range of books. Knows that information can be retrieved from books and computers.

Early learning goal – reading

Children read and understand simple sentences. They use phonic knowledge to decode regular words and read them aloud accurately. They also read some common irregular words. They demonstrate understanding when talking with others about what they have read.

Writing

Age	Typical behaviour
Birth to 11 months 8 to 20 months 16 to 26 months	Children's later writing is based on skills and understandings which they develop as babies and toddlers. Before they can write, they need to learn to use spoken language to communicate. Later they learn to write down the words they can say. Early mark-making is not the same as writing. It is a sensory and physical experience for babies and toddlers, which they do not yet connect to forming symbols which can communicate meaning.
22 to 36 months	Distinguishes between the different marks they make.
30 to 50 months	Sometimes gives meaning to marks as they draw and paint. Ascribes meanings to marks that they see in different places
40 to 60+ months	Gives meaning to marks they make as they draw, write and paint. Begins to break the flow of speech into words. Continues a rhyming string. Hears and says the initial sound in words. Can segment the sounds in simple words and blend them together. Links sounds to letters, naming and sounding the letters of the alphabet. Uses some clearly identifiable letters to communicate meaning, representing some sounds correctly and in sequence. Writes own name and other things such as labels, captions. Attempts to write short sentences in meaningful contexts.

Early learning goal – writing

Children use their phonic knowledge to write words in ways which match their spoken sounds. They also write some irregular common words. They write simple sentences which can be read by themselves and others. Some words are spelt correctly and others are phonetically plausible.

5. Mathematics

The tables below set out what you should be observing a child doing at each stage, if they are developing typically for their age.

Numbers

Age	Typical behaviour
Birth to 11 months	Notices changes in number of objects/images or sounds in group of up to 3.
8 to 20 months	Develops an awareness of number names through their enjoyment of action rhymes and songs that relate to their experience of numbers. Has some understanding that things exist, even when out of sight.
16 to 26 months	Knows that things exist, even when out of sight. Beginning to organise and categorise objects, e.g. putting all the teddy bears together or teddies and cars in separate piles. Says some counting words randomly.
22 to 36 months	Selects a small number of objects from a group when asked, for example, 'please give me one', 'please give me two'. Recites some number names in sequence. Creates and experiments with symbols and marks representing ideas of number. Begins to make comparisons between quantities. Uses some language of quantities, such as 'more' and 'a lot'. Knows that a group of things changes in quantity when something is added or taken away.

30 to 50 months	Uses some number names and number language spontaneously. Uses some number names accurately in play. Recites numbers in order to 10. Knows that numbers identify how many objects are in a set. Beginning to represent numbers using fingers, marks on paper or pictures. Sometimes matches numeral and quantity correctly. Shows curiosity about numbers by offering comments or asking questions. Compares two groups of objects, saying when they have the same number. Shows an interest in number problems. Separates a group of three or four objects in different ways, beginning to recognise that the total is still the same. Shows an interest in numerals in the environment. Shows an interest in representing numbers. Realises not only objects, but anything can be counted,
40 to 60+ months	Recognise some numerals of personal significance. Recognises numerals 1 to 5. Counts up to three or four objects by saying one number name for each item. Counts actions or objects which cannot be moved. Counts objects to 10, and beginning to count beyond 10. Counts out up to six objects from a larger group. Selects the correct numeral to represent 1 to 5, then 1 to 10objects. Counts an irregular arrangement of up to ten objects. Estimates how many objects they can see and checks by counting them. Uses the language of 'more' and 'fewer' to compare two sets of objects. Finds the total number of items in two groups by counting all of them. Says the number that is one more than a given number. Finds one more or one less from a group of up to five objects, then ten objects. In practical activities and discussion, beginning to use the vocabulary involved in adding and subtracting. Records, using marks that they can interpret and explain. Begins to identify own mathematical problems based on own

Early learning goal – numbers

Children count reliably with numbers from one to 20, place them in order and say which number is one more or one less than a given number. Using quantities and objects, they add and subtract two single-digit numbers and count on or back to find the answer. They solve problems, including doubling, halving and sharing.

Shape, space and measures

Age	Typical behaviour
Birth to 11 months	Babies' early awareness of shape, space and measure grows from their sensory awareness and opportunities to observe objects and their movements, and to play and explore.
8 to 20 months	Recognises big things and small things in meaningful contexts. Gets to know and enjoy daily routines, such as getting-up time, mealtimes, nappy time, and bedtime.
16 to 26 months	Attempts, sometimes successfully, to fit shapes into spaces on inset boards or jigsaw puzzles. Uses blocks to create their own simple structures and arrangements. Enjoys filling and emptying containers. Associates a sequence of actions with daily routines. Beginning to understand that things might happen 'now'.
22 to 36 months	Notices simple shapes and patterns in pictures. Beginning to categorise objects according to properties such as shape or size. Begins to use the language of size. Understands some talk about immediate past and future, e.g. 'before', 'later' or 'soon'. Anticipates specific time-based events such as mealtimes or home time.
30 to 50 months	Shows an interest in shape and space by playing with shapes or making arrangements with objects. Shows awareness of similarities of shapes in the environment. Uses positional language. Shows interest in shape by sustained construction activity or by talking about shapes or arrangements. Shows interest in shapes in the environment. Uses shapes appropriately for tasks. Beginning to talk about the shapes of everyday objects, e.g. 'round' and 'tall'

40 to 60+ months	Beginning to use mathematical names for 'solid' 3D shapes and 'flat' 2-D shapes, and mathematical terms to describe shapes. Selects a particular named shape. Can describe their relative position such as 'behind' or 'next to'. Orders two or three items by length or height. Orders two items by weight or capacity. Uses familiar objects and common shapes to create and recreate patterns and build models. Uses everyday language related to time. Beginning to use everyday language related to money. Orders and sequences familiar events. Measures short periods of time in simple ways.

Early learning goal – shape, space and measures

Children use everyday language to talk about size, weight, capacity, position, distance, time and money to compare quantities and objects and to solve problems. They recognise, create and describe patterns. They explore characteristics of everyday objects and shapes and use mathematical language to describe them.

6. Understanding the world

The tables below set out what you should be observing a child doing at each stage, if they are developing typically for their age.

People and communities

Age	Typical behaviour
Birth to 11 months 8 to 20 months	The beginnings of understanding of people and communities lie in early attachment and other relationships.
16 to 26 months	Is curious about people and shows interest in stories about themselves and their family. Enjoys pictures and stories about themselves, their families and other people.
22 to 36 months	Has a sense of own immediate family and relations. In pretend play, imitates everyday actions and events from own family and cultural background, e.g. making and drinking tea. Beginning to have their own friends. Learns that they have similarities and differences that connect them to, and distinguish them from, others.

30 to 50 months	Shows interest in the lives of people who are familiar to them. Remembers and talks about significant events in their own experiences. Recognises and describes special times or events for family or friends. Shows interest in different occupations and ways of life. Knows some of the things that make them unique, and can talk about some of the similarities and differences in relation to friends or family.
40 to 60+ months	Enjoys joining in with family customs and routines.

Early learning goal – people and communities

Children talk about past and present events in their own lives and in the lives of family members. They know that other children don't always enjoy the same things, and are sensitive to this. They know about similarities and differences between themselves and others, and among families, communities and traditions.

The world

Age	Typical behaviour
Birth to 11 months	Moves eyes, then head, to follow moving objects. Reacts with abrupt change when a face or object suddenly disappears from view. Looks around a room with interest; visually scans environment for novel, interesting objects and events. Smiles with pleasure at recognisable playthings. Repeats actions that have an effect, e.g. kicking or hitting a mobile or shaking a rattle.
8 to 20 months	Closely observes what animals, people and vehicles do. Watches toy being hidden and tries to find it. Looks for dropped objects. Becomes absorbed in combining objects, e.g. banging two objects or placing objects into containers. Knows things are used in different ways, e.g. a ball for rolling or throwing, a toy car for pushing.
16 to 26 months	Explores objects by linking together different approaches: shaking, hitting, looking, feeling, tasting, mouthing, pulling, turning and poking. Remembers where objects belong. Matches parts of objects that fit together, e.g. puts lid on T eapot.
22 to 36 months	Enjoys playing with small-world models such as a farm, a garage, or a train track. Notices detailed features of objects in their environment.

30 to 50 months	Comments and asks questions about aspects of their familiar world such as the place where they live or the natural world. Can talk about some of the things they have observed such as plants, animals, natural and found objects. Talks about why things happen and how things work. Developing an understanding of growth, decay and changes over time. Shows care and concern for living things and the environment.
40 to 60+ months	Looks closely at similarities, differences, patterns and change.

Early learning goal – the world

Children know about similarities and differences in relation to places, objects, materials and living things. They talk about the features of their own immediate environment and how environments might vary from one another. They make observations of animals and plants and explain why some things occur, and talk about changes.

Technology

Age	Typical behaviour
Birth to 11 months 8 to 20 months	The beginnings of understanding technology lie in babies exploring and making sense of objects and how they behave.
16 to 26 months	Anticipates repeated sounds, sights and actions, e.g. when 16 to 26 months an adult demonstrates an action toy several times. Shows interest in toys with buttons, flaps and simple mechanisms and beginning to learn to operate them.
22 to 36 months	Seeks to acquire basic skills in turning on and operating equipment. Operates mechanical toys, e.g. turns the knob on a wind-up toy or pulls back on a friction car.
30 to 50 months	Knows how to operate simple equipment. Shows an interest in technological toys with knobs or pulleys, or real objects. Shows skill in making toys work by pressing parts or lifting flaps to achieve effects such as sound, movements or new images. Knows that information can be retrieved from computers.
40 to 60+ months	Completes a simple program on a computer. Interacts with age-appropriate computer software.

Early learning goal – technology

Children recognise that a range of technology is used in places such as homes and schools. They select and use technology for particular purposes.

7. Expressive arts and design

The tables below sets out what you should be observing a child doing at each stage if they are developing typically for their age.

Exploring and using media and materials

Birth to 11 months	Babies explore media and materials as part of their exploration of the world around them.
8 to 20 months	Explores and experiments with a range of media through sensory exploration, and using whole body.
16 to 26 months	Move their whole bodies to sounds they enjoy, such as music or a regular beat. Imitates and improvises actions they have observed, e.g. clapping or waving. Begins to move to music, listen to or join in rhymes or songs. Notices and is interested in the effects of making movements which leave marks.
22 to 36 months	Joins in singing favourite songs. Creates sounds by banging, shaking, tapping or blowing. Shows an interest in the way musical instruments sound. Experiments with blocks, colours and marks.
30 to 50 months	Enjoys joining in with dancing and ring games. Sings a few familiar songs. Beginning to move rhythmically. Imitates movement in response to music. Taps out simple repeated rhythms. Explores and learns how sounds can be changed. Explores colour and how colours can be changed. Understands that they can use lines to enclose a space, and then begin to use these shapes to represent objects. Beginning to be interested in and describe the texture of things. Uses various construction materials. Beginning to construct, stacking blocks vertically and horizontally, making enclosures and creating spaces. Joins construction pieces together to build and balance. Realises tools can be used for a purpose.

40 to 60+ months	Begins to build a repertoire of songs and dances. Explores the different sounds of instruments. Explores what happens when they mix colours. Experiments to create different textures. Understands that different media can be combined to create new effects. Manipulates materials to achieve a planned effect. Constructs with a purpose in mind, using a variety of resources. Uses simple tools and techniques competently and appropriately. Selects appropriate resources and adapts work where necessary. Selects tools and techniques needed to shape, assemble and join materials they are using.

Early learning goal – exploring and using media and materials

Children sing songs, make music and dance, and experiment with ways of changing them. They safely use and explore a variety of materials, tools and techniques, experimenting with colour, design, texture, form and function.

Being imaginative

Birth to 11 months 8 to 20 months	Babies and toddlers need to explore the world and develop a range of ways to communicate before they can express their own ideas through arts and design.
16 to 26 months	Expresses self through physical action and sound. Pretends that one object represents another, especially when objects have characteristics in common.
22 to 36 months	Beginning to use representation to communicate, e.g. drawing a line and saying 'That's me'. Beginning to make-believe by pretending.

30 to 50 months	Developing preferences for forms of expression. Uses movement to express feelings. Creates movement in response to music. Sings to self and makes up simple songs. Makes up rhythms. Notices what adults do, imitating what is observed and then doing it spontaneously when the adult is not there. Engages in imaginative role-play based on own first-hand experiences. Builds stories around toys, e.g. farm animals needing rescue from an armchair 'cliff'. Uses available resources to create props to support role- play. Captures experiences and responses with a range of media, such as music, dance and paint and other materials or words.
40 to 60+ months	Create simple representations of events, people and objects. Initiates new combinations of movement and gesture in order to express and respond to feelings, ideas and experiences. Chooses particular colours to use for a purpose. Introduces a storyline or narrative into their play. Plays alongside other children who are engaged in the same theme. Plays cooperatively as part of a group to develop and act out a narrative.

Early learning goal – being imaginative

Children use what they have learnt about media and materials in original ways, thinking about uses and purposes. They represent their own ideas, thoughts and feelings through design and technology, art, music, dance, role play and stories.

This document is available for download at www.gov.uk/government/publications.